250

AUDEN AND AFTER

The Liberation of Poetry
1930–1941

AUDEN AND AFTER

The Liberation of Poetry
1930–1941

By

FRANCIS SCARFE

LONDON
GEORGE ROUTLEDGE & SONS LTD.
BROADWAY HOUSE: 68–74 CARTER LANE, E.C.

First published . *July 1942*
Second Impression . *August 1942*
Third Impression . *May 1943*
Fourth Impression January 1944
Fifth Impression February 1945
Sixth Impression . *October 1947*

Printed in Great Britain
by T. and A. CONSTABLE LTD., Hopetoun Street,
Printers to the University of Edinburgh

DEDICATORY POEM

To you, my friends
By my lamp in the evenings,
Whose words refresh
My nights, my mornings;
A doomed generation
Seized between wars,
Whose boyhood language
Was hunger and loss:
Thanks for your verses
That enrich memory
Like smiling faces
Of women and children.

All I can say
Will do you less good
Than a peaceful day
In a summer wood:
All I can give
Is a prose love,
Locked in a book
My kindest look.

F. S.

CONTENTS

PORTRAITS

INTRODUCTION

I

It might seem odd, to some readers, to present so many separate essays on such young poets, some of them immature, and call it a book. To this there are several answers. It is my belief that writers, and especially poets, must be considered as individuals and not merely as parts of groups and movements. And though the essay method has disadvantages, anyone familiar with Remy de Gourmont's 'Le Livre des Masques' and Arthur Symons's 'The Symbolist Movement in Literature', which were also written in essay form, will realize that I have tried to do for the poets of my own generation what they did for theirs. If the essays in their present form do not appear sufficiently linked together, that is because my mobilization has prevented me from adding an introductory essay to each section, as I had intended doing. And if the poets are young, that does not mean that their work is unworthy of consideration. It means, of course, that I have taken the risk of some of these poets failing to develop later, but that is their own affair rather than mine. Since the period 1929 to 1941 represents a fairly closed period, in which all these poets of 'The War Generation' (the children of the last war and the conscripts of this) made their first appearance as writers, in order to give a fairly complete idea of their direction it was necessary to include as many of them as possible. I regret to say that owing to circumstances many poets whom I admire have been omitted.

II

What I have called 'The War Generation' started producing work of public interest in 1929, when the eldest of them included here, Cecil Day Lewis, published his 'Transitional Poem', which was shortly followed by work by Auden and Spender. I have distinguished in this book four main groups among the writers with whom I have been concerned: the Auden group which includes Spender, Lewis and Macneice; the 'New Verse' group led by Grigson, and which was closely identified with the Auden group; the 'Twentieth Century Verse' group under Julian Symons, which includes such younger intellectuals as Woodcock and Mallalieu who represent a slight reaction away from New Verse; and finally, a rather heterogeneous group of sensualists, mystics and romantic extremists ranging from Dylan Thomas to the neo-Surrealists and the Apocalypse.

Of these, the 'New Verse' group is the least easy to define, for 'New Verse', so pugnaciously edited by Grigson, was so catholic as to print poets of all these groups; 'Twentieth Century Verse' also printed poets of both 'New Verse' and the 'Apocalypse', while 'Poetry' (London) is an open platform for poets of all types.

Historically, the more distinct phases might be marked by the following dates:

1929. Day Lewis's 'Transitional Poem'.

1930. Auden's 'Poems' (Faber and Faber).

1932. Michael Roberts's anthology, 'New Signatures' (Hogarth).

1933. Foundation of 'New Verse'.

First volumes of Dylan Thomas, Barker and Gascoyne.

1936. Foundation of 'Contemporary Poetry and Prose' (Roger Roughton), a Left and neo-Surrealist magazine.

1937. Foundation of 'Twentieth Century Verse' (Julian Symons).

1939. Publication of the first Apocalypse anthology, 'The New Apocalypse' (The Fortune Press).

1939. Foundation of 'Poetry' (London), by Tambi-muttu.

Besides these reviews, such reviews as 'New Writing' and 'Horizon', 'Now' and 'Kingdom Come' have also enabled the poets to widen their public in spite of the war. But anyone wanting to find a good basis for studying the first phase of the writing of this 'War Generation', that is, the 'thirties, would find the best basis in the files of 'New Verse'. There is one difficulty, however. It is that the increasingly doctrinal function of 'New Verse' meant that, in many cases, only one side of these poets' work was presented by Grigson. Therefore, in writing this book I have been at pains to buy and read thoroughly, as far as possible, the entire printed work of each author on whom I have written an essay. This meant, naturally, arriving at very different conclusions about them than could have been gained merely from study of their work in reviews.

III

Instead of approaching the poetry of the 'thirties decade in an historical manner, I have tried to approach it analytically (not in the purely appreciative spirit of Remy de Gourmont), basing my methods of criticism on two factors. The first is one imposed on me, years ago, by a phrase of T. S. Eliot's, which was something like

'Everyone talks of Poetry, but no one offers us a poem'. I have, therefore, tried to base all observations, as far as possible, on actual quotations. As for method, mine is largely the analytical method of the French 'lecture expliquée', but I have enlarged it in the direction of psychology and politics (see, for instance, the essays on Thomas and Spender) whenever the necessity arose. I do not believe that an exclusively aesthetic standard of criticism, or a grammatical and linguistic one such as the French, can be very satisfactory; such a method exclusively used would, for instance, lead to rating a poet like Ruthven Todd or Julian Symons higher than a less 'pure' poet than Dylan Thomas, whereas it is evident, on broader considerations, that he is more of a poet than either of them. At the same time, I have also tried in each case to concentrate on the positive, not the negative aspects of each man's work. Macneice once wrote that the best criticism is always 'negative'. After reading the criticism of Baudelaire and Taine I do not believe this to be always the case. It is for this reason that the most negative essay in this book, that on Auden, I find least satisfactory. It has proved negative, in spite of my admiration for Auden, because for lack of space I was obliged to select, and concentrated on his psychology and politics.

IV

In general, if there are contradictions in this book, that is largely due to the fact that in the course of the year in which these essays were written (the first written was that on Dylan Thomas, and the last on Day Lewis) I was seeking for a method of criticism, so that in the process the emphasis has gradually been shifted. None the less, I believe this analytical and individualist approach

has not prevented one fundamental fact from emerging.
It is that during the 'thirties a battle was waged among
these young poets round two opposing conceptions of
poetry; those sometimes called classical and romantic, or
cultural and emotional, or cerebral and sensual. The
Auden group especially, strongly influenced by T. S.
Eliot, turned to the seventeenth century for a guide;
they admired Donne and Dryden and believed in absolute
scales of value. They were actively engaged in politics
and gave their poetry a decided social bias. They tried
to write in the language of common speech; they tried
to be scientific (such an image as Charles Madge's 'Like
the dark germs across the filter clean' would have
delighted Pope or Voltaire), and they tried to be 'direct'.
Similar claims to objectivity were made by Grigson and
most of the 'New Verse' group, who adopted a phrase
of Auden's about poets being 'reporters' (Julian Symons
enlarged this very well to 'every poet is an *unconscious*
mass-observer'), and the best statement of this conception of poetry, which is a perfectly legitimate one,
though to my mind limited, has been made by Grigson
himself: 'I always judge poetry, first, by its relation to
current speech, the language in which one is angry about
Spain or in which one is pleasant or unpleasant to one's
wife. I judge every poem written now, by poets under
forty, by the degree to which it takes notice, for ends not
purely individual, of the universe of objects and events.'
As I have been myself influenced by 'New Verse', my
practice is often very close to this statement of Grigson's,
but at the same time it obviously needs enlarging, if the
younger poets are to be properly understood. The sense
in which I would enlarge it is indicated in the 'Letter
on Poetry' at the end of this book. But Grigson was
not the only legislator of poetry who tended to be severe:
Symons was always rapping young poets over the knuckles

for being 'careless' or 'formless', owing, I think, to his very arbitrary conception of form. In spite of all their arbitrary ideas, these poets of the war generation are as far from being 'classical' as the man in the moon. This is a fundamentally romantic generation, filled with immense ideals for peace and social progress, and above all, with a great mythological conception of themselves as martyrs, born into one war and fattened for another. They also lived in a period socially and intellectually too muddled for them to hope to be classical in any way, for classicism only emerges in periods of stability, both social and cultural. We cannot accept the superficial 'classicism' of Gautier, from which Macneice for instance is not far removed, as the real thing. How could these poets hope to reconcile their Donne, Dryden and Dante with Rilke, Freud and Marx? They never really digested them. What they did digest thoroughly was the work of their immediate predecessors, those poets now in or almost in their 'fifties, such as Pound, Eliot, Herbert Read, Edwin Muir, the Sitwells, Robert Graves and D. H. Lawrence. And all these poets are far from classicism, far from any community of outlook. Individualism has been the most characteristic attitude of the modern poets as a whole.

Side by side with these would-be classical poets, there existed from 1934 onwards a great emotional revival, headed by Dylan Thomas and George Barker. These two also had contact with English neo-Surrealism in 1936 and 1937, and when the Apocalypse started in 1938, Dylan Thomas was practically its god. This battle for the liberation of emotion, and against purely intellectual and cerebral standards, which Lawrence himself had so valiantly preached, was taken up especially by Tambimuttu and his sympathizers in his review 'Poetry'. Tambimuttu has written several essays in which he

places 'emotional drive' and 'personal integrity' among
the highest qualities of the poet. Herbert Read, who,
more than any poet of his generation, has been able to
understand and follow sympathetically the work of the
younger poets, has himself written an essay pleading the
cause of anarchism and personal expression for the
younger poets. Henry Treece and J. F. Hendry are
now clamouring for a revival of myth, and a new doctrine
of expressionism. The war has weakened the position
of the 'Intellectual' poets, who had too readily com-
mitted themselves to Communism and other ready-made
ideas and systems, and has hastened the activities of the
sensualists or expressionists. There is a great possibility
that during the war, or immediately after it, the two
opposing factions might draw together. It is significant
to see that Auden, from America, in his 'New Year
Letter' is aware of the intellectual confusion of the
modern world, that he is increasingly aware that the
individual must solve his own problems if he wants to
help society as a whole, and that he is returning rapidly
to his original doctrine of 'a change of heart' which he
first propounded in 1930. It is significant that Spender
has recently produced an appreciative essay on Shelley;
that Macneice has shown a profound understanding of
that great Romantic, Yeats; that Allott, whose ideas
seemed so cut and dried, has during the war published
an excellent book on Jules Verne; that Ruthven Todd is
finishing a book on Blake, and that Day Lewis has
translated that most florid of works, Virgil's 'The
Georgics'. In other terms, the battle of the classical-
romantic or objective-subjective among the younger
poets has been largely one of artificial differences and
abstractions, and in reality there is not much fundamental
difference between them.

The main task lying before these poets after the war

is to modify the arbitrariness of their outlooks and find some more generous conception of 'thought' and 'feeling'. This can only be done by taking the most inclusive conception of each, and not by making narrow 'School' programmes. And another great work to be continued is that of making poetry, in range and idiom, more accessible to the masses than it has ever been.

FRANCIS SCARFE.

UNIVERSITY OF GLASGOW,
    August 1941.

NOTE TO INTRODUCTION

Since the above was written several changes have been made in this book. Six short essays have been omitted (on Roy Fuller, H. B. Mallalieu, Gavin Ewart, D. S. Savage, George Woodcock and Tambimuttu). I shall no doubt write about these elsewhere at a later date. Three essays have been added: on Louis Macneice, 'Observations on Poetry and War' and 'The Liberation of Poetry'. These essays have been written under rather unusual conditions, but if the army provides little scope for writing it also provides much time for thought, and it is hoped that they might contribute something positive to the questions raised.

In the process of revision it has been noticed that there is some repetition of ideas from one essay to another. It is emphasized that this is not accidental: each essay can be read as a separate unit, and the reader is under no obligation to begin at page one and read through to the end: but if there is any unity it should lie in the way various aspects of a problem might be treated from one essay to another. La Bruyère once wrote that a book should be constructed as one constructs a clock; that is not the case here, for, while some of the essays (for instance, that on Dylan Thomas) were thus constructed, the book as a whole, like Topsy, 'just grew'. If signs of an unruly mind have occasionally intruded, I apologize; but with no shame, since this book has for me been a sort of testament, written:

> En l'an trentiesme de mon aage
> Que toutes mes hontes j'ay bues.

FRANCIS SCARFE.

R.A.O.C.
December 1941.

ACKNOWLEDGMENTS are due to the Editor of 'Horizon' for permission to reprint the essay on Dylan Thomas from 'Horizon', October 1940; and to Tambimuttu for permission to print the 'Letter on Poetry' which was to have appeared in 'Poetry' (London).

Acknowledgments are due to the following publishers for quotations from works printed by them: Faber & Faber (Auden, Spender, Macneice, Barker, Eliot); J. M. Dent (Dylan Thomas and Hugh Sykes Davies); Parton Press (Barker, Thomas, Gascoyne); Fortune Press (Symons, Nicholas Moore, Treece, Hendry, Fraser, Waller, Apocalypse); Hogarth Press (Allott, Day Lewis); Chatto & Windus (Prokosch); Jonathan Cape (Day Lewis); Routledge (The White Horseman); Cresset Press (Grigson). Also for photographs to Messrs. J. M. Dent (Dylan Thomas), Jonathan Cape (Cecil Day Lewis) and Chatto & Windus (Frederic Prokosch).

Further acknowledgments are due to the Editors of the following periodicals: 'New Verse', 'Twentieth Century Verse', 'Poetry' (London), 'Contemporary Poetry and Prose', 'New Writing', 'Horizon', 'Now', 'Seven', 'Wales', etc.

THE DEVELOPMENT OF DAY LEWIS

LIKE Auden, Day Lewis is a deceptive poet, with a great deal of irrelevance in his work, but beneath it some solid virtues. He has sometimes been described as a Georgian gone wrong, and it is certain that in spirit he does not quite belong to the Auden group with which he has been associated. But he is a Georgian with a difference, a Georgian who has read Eliot, Hopkins and Marx—and that means a great deal.

Lewis has been a slow developer as a poet, and it is hard, at the present time, when comparing his later with his earlier work, to understand why his 'Transitional Poem' and 'From Feathers to Iron' were so wildly acclaimed ten years ago. It was, I think, because he came forward at the right time with a concrete enthusiasm, with an overwhelming desire to create and defend something constructive. This was a new note after the decade of despondency which had followed on 'The Waste Land'.

'Transitional Poem' (1929) was anything but a flying start. At that time all the young poets were modelling themselves on Eliot, and Lewis was among them, but only in a mild way. This mild way was in imitating the new fashion of adding pedantic notes to his otherwise inoffensive poems. These notes were stuffed with Spinoza, Dante and Donne, with a little Wyndham Lewis and Sophie Tucker thrown in as light refreshment. The name of Wyndham Lewis is significant. This explains a great deal of the 'toughness' and the air of positiveness which have been maintained by Day Lewis ever since his earliest works. The main Note is important: 'The central theme of this poem is the single mind. The poem is divided into four parts, which essentially represent

A

four phases of single-mindedness: it will be seen that a transition is intended from one part to the next such as implies a certain spiritual progress and a constant shifting of aspect. As far as any definitions can be attached to these aspects, they may be termed (1) metaphysical, (2) ethical, (3) psychological, while (4) is an attempt to relate the poetic impulse with the experience as a whole. Formally, the parts fall with fair accuracy into the divisions of a theorem in geometry, i.e. general enunciation, particular enunciation, proof, corollaries . . . etc.'

It is to be regretted that, with all these intentions, the poem is far from being as logical or as compactly built as the note suggests: anyone reading it without this note might regard it only as the usual type of miscellaneous collection of poems. In any case, if there is a main subject, it is rather different from, and more important than, the note suggests. In the first poem he writes:

> It is certain we shall attain
> No life until we stamp on all
> Life the tetragonal
> Pure symmetry of brain.

In the second part, Lewis does not particularize this general theme. Instead, a tense struggle seems to develop, when the poet considers in many of its aspects, not the problem of 'single-mindedness' so much as the problem of sensuality. Though some of this is presented in rather a silly way—

> The man who nuzzles
> In a woman's lap
> Burrows towards a night
> Too deep for puzzles

—there is a characteristic honesty, and a hint of Lewis's later power, in

> It seems that we must call
> Anything truth whose well

CECIL DAY LEWIS

> Is deep enough;
> For the essential
> Philosopher-stone, desire,
> Needs no other proof
> Than its own fire.

This is admirably written, and the clipped effect of these short lines, the directness of the statement itself, shows clearly that Lewis was striving after a concise style with no frills. The main point here is that, after fourteen poems, the poet has contradicted his first premiss. After two more he goes even farther, writing:

> Let logic analyse the hive,
> Wisdom's content to have the honey.

The first quality of Day Lewis is his good sense.

The Third Part of the 'Transitional Poem' is a chaos of personal experiences, many of them too recondite to be of immediate interest. This part is an assertion of individualism, and as such does not seem to emerge logically from the previous poems:

> Mine is the heron's flight
> Which makes a solitude of any sky.

This, again, is excellent: it is also, in conjunction with the kestrel image used in later poems, another indication of Lewis's point of contact with the Auden–Spender group, the conflict between individual- and mass-salvation.

The Fourth Part, which aims at so much, with its supposed presentation of corollaries, is also very chaotic, but tense in spite of occasional rhetoric. One of the most important points made, since it defines and characterizes all Lewis's subsequent work, is to be found, however inadequately expressed, in Poem 33:

> I stretched a line from pole to pole
> To hang my paper lanterns on.   Poor soul,
> By such a metaphysical conceit
> Thinking to make ends meet!

This line, spun from the blind heart—
What could it do but prove the poles apart ?
More expert now, I twist the dials, catch
Electric hints, curt omens such
As may be heard by one tapping the air
That belts an ambiguous sphere.
Put down the tripod here.

It is evident that Lewis saw the weakness of all intellectual attempts to solve anything by abstract logic alone: this amounts to a refutal of his Euclidian conception of his first long poem, and decides a new direction for his work: that of basing all his judgments of life and human nature on the study of concrete instances and living men. And in fact there is as much difference between his conception of poetry in 1929 and that which he arrived at by 1935 as there is between telepathy and wireless.

The 'Transitional Poem' is one of the strangest poems of the 'thirties, since it is the product of one of the strangest minds. This Poem 33 especially is an image in miniature of his future work. Consider, for a moment, his characteristic titles: 'Transitional Poem'; 'From Feathers to Iron'; 'The Magnetic Mountain'; 'A Time to Dance'; 'Overtures to Death'; 'Starting Point'. They show Lewis as having a sort of Kafka uneasiness, an urgent desire always to be going somewhere else or beginning something new. This is typical of the English romantic conception of space, that thought 'If anything goes wrong I'll go to America', or 'Perhaps I would be better off in Australia'. (This is what led, says one of my friends, to the British Empire, where people went not so as to make something better, but merely to escape from Britain.) Secondly, this desire for movement is paralleled by a constant preoccupation with the hardness, the resistance of matter. We find in the 'Transitional Poem' dozens of instances of this: for example—'Strata undiagnosed'; 'love's geology'; 'basalt peace'; 'authority of ice'; 'where is the true the central stone'; 'jag of sense'; 'hammered out on lead'; 'Himalayas of the mind'; 'muscular stream'; 'digest an adamant'. There are dozens more, which are completed in the obsession with mountains and hills, which later gave its title to 'The Magnetic Mountain'. Beside this idea of solidness, there is another constant image in Lewis which is of great interest. In his earlier poems especially he is obsessed by the image of flying sparks (a psycho-analyst would call it an obsession with sperm), and this flying spark later crystallizes in the numerous electricity images, the 'electric hints' quoted above becoming a full conception of electricity with all its attendant metaphors—'When the charged batteries of desire', etc. These basic images, the one type of solidity and immobility, the other type of instability and movement, reunite very well in the later poems with their imagery of turbines, girders, cantilever bridges, wires, pylons and wheels. This mechanical imagery can sometimes be overdone, but it is a mistake to believe, as some critics have believed, that this is in any way superficial or affected. Lewis, to my mind, is not merely being schoolboyish or trying to be 'tough', but this type of imagery is fundamental to his conception of the modern world. And that this was all latent in the 'Transitional Poem' is a fact which refutes those critics who have said that Lewis owes all his 'modern dress' to Auden. Such signs as there are of Auden in this poem are very slight indeed. His basic imagery is indicative of his own, and no other poet's, neurosis. When he developed it later, he gave it a more positive value by using it in a social context.

Having said so much, there is little need for a detailed analysis of Lewis's later work. His development has been

logical, and not disappointing. Although he has occasionally written nonsense such as 'Grecians awake, salute
the happy norm' and the poem 'Take a whole holiday
in honour of this', by the time he reached the 'Overtures
to Death' he had practically subdued this weakness, save
for an occasional reference to death in an Audenesque
or Wyndham Lewis manner as 'bailiff' and 'Mister'.

The theme of 'From Feathers to Iron' was the
approaching birth of a child, and within its limits the
subject was better treated than in the 'Transitional
Poem', as well as allowing a wider range of reference.
Here the most permanent side of Lewis's work makes its
appearance: those excellent lyrics about love and nature.

In these lyrics, Lewis is a far more sympathetic person
than in those other poems in which he is a boyish
Hemingway with an unnatural veneer of toughness: he
can write:

> Now she is like the white rose-tree
> That takes a blessing from the sun;
> Summer has filled her veins with light,
> And her warm blood is washed with noon;

or:

> Now the full-throated daffodils,
> Our trumpeters in gold,
> Call resurrection from the ground
> And bid the year be bold.

The only defect in some of the lyrics is their sudden
and ill-judged change of tone, as in the poem which
begins 'Come as the wind is whirling our summer away'
and ends with a catalogue of insulators, turbines and
freight.

'The Magnetic Mountain' shows a further development
in both tone and idiom. By this time Lewis had fallen
more under Auden's influence and had re-read Hopkins.

There was also a change of direction. Lewis, as the above quotations show, is primarily an exultant poet with an immense gusto. In 'The Magnetic Mountain' this gusto, fully realized in his images of kestrel, bridges, furnaces and pistons, is now deadened by a gloomy note which seems less natural and less spontaneous. It is the gloom of an optimist at a funeral, feeling it his duty to pull a long face. This is found in certain ominous poems and threatening lines like

> Positively, this is the end of the track.
> It's rather late and there's no way back.

This was a rather distressing way of imitating Auden. Most of the poems in 'The Magnetic Mountain' show Lewis continually whipping up an immense hustle and bustle of departure to the Mountain—

> Then I'll hit the trail for that promising land,
> May catch up with Wystan and Rex, my friend

—which gave the impression of a Sunday School treat and the Salvation Army let loose. This excitement was inevitably followed by fits of depression, gloomy tags of mass-observation which only ended in another fit of bustle. Someone has said the Magnetic Mountain was Auden. It might also have been a father-complex similar to Wordsworth's, who was also obsessed by mountains. On the immediate surface, the Mountain is more obviously Communism and the Communist State; and, whether by coincidence or design, the Mountain recalls the image of La Montagne, which was the first name of the great revolutionary mass of Jacobins in the early years of the French Revolution. 'The Magnetic Mountain', with all its exuberant faults, was certainly the heartiest piece of Left propaganda written in the 'thirties. It is more exhilarating on a first reading than on the second. But its lyrical parts had great moving power, and have so still.

Since 'The Magnetic Mountain', two important things have happened to Day Lewis as a poet. First of all, he has established himself as a narrative poet. Both his long poem about Airmen and 'The Loss of The Nabara' are overlaid with description, but the latter can compete with the best naval narratives in our language. This poem is not sufficiently well known. Of all the poems produced about the Spanish war, many of them, like Auden's and Barker's, on a high emotional level, this is the only solid narrative, and written with sustained feeling:

> Canarias, though easily she out-paced and out-gunned
>   her,
> Finding this midge could sting,
> Edged off, and beneath a wedge of smoke steamed in a ring
> On the rim of the trawler's range, a circular storm of
>   thunder.
> But always Nabara turned her broadside, manœuvring
> To keep both guns on the target, scorning safety devices.
> Slow now the battle's tempo, irregular the beat
> Of gunfire in the heart
> Of the afternoon, the distempered sky sank to the crisis,
> Shell-shocked the sea tossed and hissed in delirious heat. . . .

The poem is so much an organic whole, and heroic in the best sense, that no isolated quotation can adequately convey its power. This is a line which Lewis will probably develop increasingly, and for which his translation of 'The Georgics' (though his style as a translator is heavier than his own style) has more fully prepared him.

The second important development is that, without losing his rather Priestley-like solidness and common sense, Lewis is becoming less aggressive and can present an argument more concisely than ever before. This is to be seen especially in the half-dozen lyrics he has contributed to numbers of 'The Penguin New Writing' during the war. The Communist of yesterday, now rather chastened and a member of the Home Guard, has summed up his outlook on the situation perfectly well in his short poem 'Where are the War Poets?':

> It is the logic of our times,
> No subject for immortal verse,
> That we who lived by honest dreams
> Defend the bad against the worse.

This power of epigrammatic writing completes that richer descriptive power he attained in 'The Nabara', and the spirit of the poem quoted above is fairly representative of the younger poets' spontaneous reaction to the war. For they are determined that things will have to be better after the war than they were before. I must confess that until I wrote this essay, in rather a hurry in the few days remaining to me, I was more indifferent to Lewis's work than I am now. I find in it, reading it for perhaps the last time, a deep integrity and a firm attachment to the best human aspirations, as well as a growing and now mature ability to express them.

August 1941.

ASPECTS OF AUDEN:

THE 'ENFANT TERRIBLE' OF THE 'THIRTIES

I. *The Importance of Auden*

IT is well to distinguish, historically, between great poets and important poets. Among the so-called 'Metaphysicals' there was not a great poet: there was, however, at least one poet of importance, Donne. The Metaphysicals as a whole are a good illustration of the fact that the climate of poetry at any time is not decided by the great poet, but by the level of the work of its minor poets. The Metaphysicals were a group of minor poets whose work was homogeneous and on a consistent level of integrity, but among them only Donne is important. The importance of a poet depends not so much on the quality or quantity of his work as on its power of radiation: Donne seems to be the most typical of his generation, both in their faults and virtues, which he stylized. He had, himself, both a limited range of expression and a very narrow outlook when compared with his great predecessors, Spenser, Marlowe, Shakespeare. But Donne digested and concentrated a great deal of the tumultuous and haphazard achievement of the Renaissance.

Blake, again, is no great poet, but an important one. A smaller poet than Wordsworth, a weaker thinker than Coleridge, a less competent craftsman than Shelley, he gives better than any of them a mirror of the disintegration and idealism of his times, and is more modern than any of these three poets.

W. H. Auden will also be an important poet. He is a poet who is destined to miss greatness, but who might achieve importance by his synthesis of the typical thought

[*Photo Eric Bramall, A.R.P.S.*

W. H. AUDEN

and practice of poetry of his own time. But Spender might yet prove a greater poet: while the place of 'important' poet might well be wrested from him by T. S. Eliot. Eliot is unquestionably a finer poet and a better craftsman, with better taste, a more sane sense of proportion and a firmer control of language. Indeed, Auden owes many of his best qualities to Eliot. Auden has no individual poem which can rival 'Prufrock', 'Ash Wednesday', 'The Waste Land', 'East Coker', 'Dry Salvages', unless it be his poem 'Spain', which would give Eliot a score of five to one against Auden. This is a crude method of assessment, but any reader knowing the two poets will agree that with this quantitive estimate are implied also the great variations of method and style which are covered in Eliot's five poems. Nor has Auden done anything in the drama which, to my mind, Eliot has not done.

The main problem, though, in comparing these two poets, is one of direction. Auden is more modern in all those elements which a purely social criticism would exalt: his poetry is a clearing-house for modern psychology and social doctrine. If Eliot seems rooted in the past, Auden is topical to a fault, but seems turned towards the future. I cannot solve this problem of their relative importance, but, reckoning Auden's youth and capacity for development, he still has his work cut out to outstrip Eliot.

Auden represents a sort of A B C of the poetry of the 'thirties, that is to say of 'The War Generation'. All that is latent in Eliot is seen developed and sometimes rotten-ripe in him. And all his faults are implicit in the term a 'contemporary' poet; the cheapness, the jazz, the slang, the easy thrills, the disrespect and slovenliness of a muddled age.

But now, when attempts are being made to wipe

Auden off the map of poetry, as they have wiped France off the map of culture, it is time to reaffirm that Auden corresponds to a real phase and state of mind in his generation; that there is hardly a young poet who is not in some way indebted to him; that there are some things in which he excels, such as the sensuous and tender lyric and the mocking witty satire; and that as a 'warner' he has consistently, at least until he went to America, understood the mind and aspirations of the younger generation. And we shall add that if he sometimes writes badly, it is because he writes as one who has too freely assimilated many ways of writing, and this fluency is one which springs from his very virtue of spontaneity. Even if Auden were to write no more, or to write nothing better than his turgid 'Ode to Henry James', what he wrote before 1940 would lose nothing of its importance.

I ought, I suppose, to make some justification of this emphasis on Auden's importance. In an age of muddle-headedness from which such a penetrating mind as Eliot (who had clipped the church's wings, brought his demi-mondaines, gangsters, prostitutes, commercial travellers and dissecting tables into poetry) withdrew blushing into the queasy bosom of Anglo-Catholicism, in an age of hypocrisy, fragments and wasted energies, Auden has been the only poet (apart from Pound and Eliot) to attempt some kind of synthesis. The synthesis of Eliot and Pound was a cultural one: Auden has had the courage to face some unpleasant facts and attempt a social synthesis. Emerging from such a period, his synthesis could be nothing but odd, and a future generation is bound to regard it as rather pathetic. But he got round his problem (as Blake did) by an unusual capacity for myth-making and sheer disregard for reputation. If his poetry is in any sense good, it is not in the sense of a

modern stream-lined car, but it has the primitive, shapeless, rough-and-ready goodness of home-made bread.   In
his work, Einstein and Freud, Homer Lane and Dryden,
rub shoulders with all the realities of the life of the street,
the salon and the slum.   His poetry is very much about
'maps and chaps', and that is why it is important for us
now, even if it does not remain so.   And it has an intense
belief in the future of man which is emotionally presented.
He presents the bustle and humbug and smell of modern
life by his capacity for mythological thinking, his feeling
for all sorts of places, all sorts of people into whose life he
has not penetrated but which he intuitively understands,
his love of make-believe, his power for brutal generalization which gives point to many fragments of observation,
and gives body to his personal beliefs.

What strikes one first is his emphasis on psychology
and politics.   What lingers in the memory is his exquisite
lyrical gift, in such poems as 'O lurcher loving collier
black as night', which he has not sufficiently exploited.
The greatest fault of his work is that, like Aldous Huxley's
novels, it is full of undigested gobbets of knowledge which
can be found in any popular handbook.   And this brings
us to perhaps the worst fault that can be found in a poet:
he underestimates (like Huxley) the intelligence of his
reader.   Eliot, much wiser, has done the opposite, as has
Ezra Pound.   Only time will tell whether the seeming
pompousness of those two poets will not prove merits:
we must remember that (to all appearances) with the
broadening of education we are moving towards an
ever-widening and better-educated, or at least better-
informed, public.   And then the vice of Auden will be
even more evident than it is now, though it might be
forgiven when it co-exists with the deep feeling he
attains.

II. *Auden's Psychology*

One of the most curious things about Auden is that, in spite of his emphasis on psychology, on close examination his poetry is not particularly introspective, not so much, say, as Spender's. And it is also noticeable that while his poetry is 'about chaps', there is very little about individual chaps, and much more about people in general. The word 'I' is, strangely enough, not frequently used in his verse. There is much more of 'we' and 'they'.

The weakness of Auden's psychology is that it is too often based on sweeping generalizations. The pseudo-psychology, by which disease is represented purely as defence-mechanism and selfishness, leads Auden very often to treat suffering cruelly as though it were a joke. As for Freud, it is amusing to see that a poet who professes immense admiration for Dryden (that poet whom nobody reads, and who is out of the direct line of English poetry, and who, once again, was revived not by Auden but by Eliot, to whom he is better suited)—it is amusing to see this pseudo-classical poet, who is as different from Dryden as an octopus from a whale, holding a Freudian and ultra-romantic conception of the poet. In a long essay in 'The Arts To-day' Auden defended Freud's view of the artist as a social misfit who tries to reconcile himself with society through his art. In other terms, we are to return to Baudelaire's albatross, Shelley's stricken deer, the false Romantic conception of the artist as a crank. It would have seemed that for a near-Marxist such a conception of the poet could hardly be adequate. It would have been more logical if Auden, instead of accepting this reactionary conception of the poet, were to adopt that really progressive one of Eric Gill, according to whom the artist is merely an 'ordinary man' who happens to produce art: 'The artist is not a special kind of man, but every man is a special kind of artist.' But no, Auden is as romantic as a schoolboy, much more romantic than Spender and much less logical. I think also that Auden, like most of us, was also too ready to accept the overemphasis on sex for which we must blame all lay disciples of Freud. In any case, Auden's use of sexual symbolism is commonplace, when compared with that of Dylan Thomas. Indeed, in comparing the sexual symbolism of these two poets we see how far removed Auden is from having *seen the world in sexual terms* (as Thomas has): that is to say, he has appropriated the lessons of Freud, but not assimilated them or found they had any deep personal meaning for himself.

I do not propose to undertake an analysis of the psychological background of Auden, feeling it would be a long task and not particularly interesting. Having partly done so for my own purposes, I should say that the overemphasis on such writers as Freud, Lane, Groddeck, with all the contradictions and get-out of special pleading implied, and the neglect of Gestalt and other contemporary theories of psychology, do seem to give some justification to the critics of the Left, who would have liked to see Auden accept a more materialist view of life, as indeed he professes to do. There were, of course, always contradictions in his application of psychological theory to poetry. In 'The Orators', for instance, when addressing schoolboys, he developed a strong attack on neurotics of all kinds, as though they were the enemies of society. It would have been more to the point to argue that these neurotics were produced by an unsatisfactory state of society. Indeed (unless I have missed the irony), the injunction to throw them 'into the black hole' is not far removed from the Nazi treatment of lunatics and incurables. Further, Auden's attitude to neurotics is in contradiction to his acceptance of the Freudian view of the artist as neurotic ; and, finally, he fails in that sympathy which is one of the prerequisites of all psycho-analytic method. If asked to justify these assertions, there is no need to confine ourselves to 'The Orators'. A major theme in 'The Ascent of F. 6' is the mother-fixation or oedipus-complex, which, far from reaching the heights of sublimity one might expect, is presented in a somewhat contemptible and ridiculous light. 'Miss Gee' is a cruel ballad written round the idea of compensation, or alternatively round the idea that growths and tumours are deliberately grown by their sufferers. 'The Orators' itself is little more than a fictional treatment of a return to normality by means of 'sublimation', but here again, in the case of the schoolboys' hero, the Airman, the cure is presented in a ridiculous light. It is unfortunate that, while possessing such a psychological background, Auden has so often misapplied it. But the misapplication is not due to a failure to understand psychology : it is due rather to a failure of sympathy. This is sometimes evident on a social plane. For instance, there is the ballad of John Honeyman, who invented an explosive and was obliged to sell it to a foreign power, the result being that he and his family were wiped out by his own invention. Here Auden laughs loudly, and we are also invited to laugh. But we reflect : the struggle for education by John Honeyman, far from being ridiculous, is pathetic, and is typical of thousands of struggling young men today. And the fact that scientific talent should be wasted in creating engines of destruction is no laughing matter. And the fact that such things can be bought and sold, and used against victims who, by force of circumstance, connived at their invention and pro-duction, is one of the greatest tragedies of modern times. No, this is a poem over which one laughs and cries twice.

But it is not my purpose, in spite of the above, to attack Auden. If misapplied, his psychology has been valuable, and he has helped us to learn how it can be assimilated to poetry. One thing about his ready use of modern psychology is that it appeals at once to a modern public who have more than a smattering of psychological theory. It caters especially for a public of introspectives, for that is almost what the modern public has become. For it is a strange thing that in an age when political feeling has run high, and there has been a determined effort at writing social, even class-literature, the greatest works have been in the main psychological. Against the social writing of Jules Romains, Dos Passos, Aragon and the collaborators of 'New Writing', must be placed the analytic work of such people as Proust, Gide, Joyce, Lawrence, Duhamel and Kafka, who are among the outstanding names of our time. Auden has a foot in both camps, but I am inclined to think that in him the psychological approach dominates his social approach to writing and to human problems. By far the most important use of his psychology is that it has gilded the pill of his Left politics. He is heading more and more towards an interpretation of political and social problems in psychological terms. It is this which explains the great amount of controversy which has raged round his politics in the last ten years. Those who thought he would interpret psychological problems in Marxist or political terms have been woefully mistaken, and it is the error of that belief which made a great deal of Left criticism of Auden out of date before it was written. Even Auden's Geography (which is one of his main assets: his poems carry us round the world in no time) is psychic, and it is his interpretation of places such as Dover,

Iceland and Spain, which led me to use the term 'Psychic Geography'.

Of all Auden's poems, 'Spain' is the most sustained and the most admirable. A close reading of this shows that here he has interpreted a political event of first importance in psychological, not political terms. After treating history as the gradual breakdown of superstition and its replacement by science, the uneasiness and unrest of the people are expressed in terms of superstition, and in terms of a father-fixation:

> And the nations combine each cry, invoking the life
> That shapes the individual belly and orders
> The private nocturnal terror:
> ' Did you not found once the city state of the sponge,

> 'Raise the vast military empires of the shark
> And the tiger, establish the robin's plucky canton?
> Intervene. O descend as a dove or
> A furious papa or a mild engineer: but descend.'

> And the life, if it answers at all, replies from the heart
> And the eyes and the lungs, from the shops and squares of
> the city:
> 'O no, I am not the Mover,
> Not to-day, not to you. To you I'm the

> 'Yes-man, the bar-companion, the easily duped:
> I am whatever you do; I am your vow to be
> Good, your humorous story;
> I am your business voice; I am your marriage.

> 'What's your proposal? To build the Just City? I will.
> I agree. Or is it the suicide-pact, the romantic
> Death? Very well, I accept, for
> I am your choice, your decision: yes, I am Spain.'

The 'cry of the nations' to some external authority is quite rightly rebuked by Auden, who replies in these lines that 'life', or 'the Mover', the shaper of human destinies, is the individual's own sense of responsibility, his own conscience. This means that Spain can only be saved by an internal effort, first of all, on the part of all those who would save her. And, indeed, the individual conscience will in its turn be uplifted or degraded by the fate of Spain. This seems an extremely ingenious application of psychology to a political problem, but it is also one of the first indications of Auden's real psychological and political direction: the direction is towards individualism: towards Anarchism, in fact. Incidentally, the above extract, which lacks that power of pageantry and concentration of the rest of this poem, gives a good indication of some of the characteristics of Auden's looser style of writing. In the first six lines, a very inadequate idea of the vast travail of life or God is given in this list of pregnancy, nightmare, and a few references to sponges, sharks and tigers. In the next few lines I think Auden's taste has failed him badly when, in the midst of one of the most serious poems he has written, he introduces a facetious element with his 'furious papa' and 'mild engineer'. This same fault occurs towards the end of the poem when he talks of the young poets 'exploding like bombs', which was scarcely a happy image. In the rest of the above passage I feel that the tone of the poem is seriously lowered, but perhaps this only enhances the effect of the brutal return to the reality of the situation, in the blunt statement: 'I am Spain'. Auden has a tendency to lapse into very casual writing at critical moments, and this is one of them. But often, as in this case, he gets away with it because in its context such a piece is embedded in very serious writing, and does not last long enough to destroy the emotional tension previously built up. Taking such pieces separately, however, they hardly bear inspection, and are the least inviting parts of Auden's work. To return to the point, even the battlefields of Spain are later presented in the poem as a sort of screen on which our own psychological disturbances are horribly projected:

> On that table-land scored by rivers
> Our fever's menacing shapes are precise and alive.

Had Auden failed to raise his psychology above a personal level it might have been dismissed as incidental trimming to his poetry. But his psychological interpretation of politics is justifiable. The chaos of the period between the two wars he completely understood in his elegy on Yeats in 1939, when he wrote:

> Intellectual disgrace
> Stares from every human face
> And the seas of pity lie
> Locked and frozen in each eye.

For the Marxist contention that all wars are purely economic in origin can quite well, and must, be completed by the realization that they also reflect the state of the human conscience. In his 'New Year Letter' Auden has more fully developed the idea of war as a symptom of maladjustments and inadequacies in us all. The problem is whether the hen came first or the egg: is it the evil in man which produces war and competition, or is it social injustice which produce these moral evils? The Marxist answer is clear: it is the environment which produces psychological disorders. Auden has a certain mysticism in his psychology: he is aware of the Marxist stand, but he seems to vacillate between that and the Freudian idea that the psychic evil produces the social evil. Some day Auden will have to make his choice, and if he makes the latter choice, he will perforce arrive at the same position which Eliot has reached by way of Christianity, which also, long before psycho-analysis, traced injustice and social evil to moral sources. But, at present, I think Auden's general position is nearer to Anarchism than to either Marxism or Christianity.

III. *Auden's Politics*

But what about Auden's politics? So much has been written on this subject that I hesitate to add my quota for or against. Philip Henderson, in his book 'The Poet and Society'—one of the few sensible studies of poetry which have been done on near-Marxist lines—came to the conclusion that Auden was merely writing 'for himself and his private friends', a conclusion which I consider very inadequate. It is true that Auden has written a good deal for himself and his friends, which he has every right to do. But I refuse to believe that a poet who could write 'Spain' is not sincerely interested in the political scene, or that he has failed to give any significant expression to his views. I leave aside the problems of his public-school education, his rather slender teaching experience, or his behaviour as a member of parties, which are his own business. Auden's poetry has always been profoundly social, concerned with man as a social creature at work and play in the twentieth century. He has bothered hardly at all about man's relation to nature, or about such end-problems as life, death, eternity, which have occupied Eliot. Even his love poems seem to be about other people: he is a poet turned outwards. It is this being 'turned outwards' which accounts for much of his sermonizing. But the word 'political' does not apply to his poetry so well as the general word 'social'.

In 'Paid on Both Sides', perhaps his most muddled and unsatisfactory work, he presented some people, about whom we learn very little, engaged in shooting each other with schoolboyish zest and remorse. There is something of Synge in this writing. These people, like Auden's generation, feel that they have unjustly inherited a tradition of violence, which they are powerless to shake off. The most significant thing in this work is that all these violent people are pacifists:

> *Tom.* I am sick of this feud. What do we want to go on
> killing each other for?
> We are all the same. He's trash, yet if I cut my
> finger it bleeds like his. . . . (p. 17)

*

> *John.* Could I have been some simpleton that lived
> Before disaster sent his runners here. . . . (p. 20)

*

> *M.* Kill him.
> *Seth.* I can't do that. There is peace now; besides, he is
> a guest in our house.
> *M.* Have you forgotten your brother's death . . . etc.
> *Seth.* I'm not afraid of anything or anybody, but I don't
> want to.
> *M.* I shall have to take steps.
> *Seth.* It shall be as you like. Though I think that much
> will come of this, chiefly harm. . . . (pp. 35-36)

There are all the possibilities of tragic development in such a situation, where men are unwillingly set to kill each other and powerless to do otherwise. But Auden is far from achieving any tragic situation in this charade, because there is no development of character no more development, in fact, than there is in any charade. What is worse, the character, where there is any, seems hopelessly superficial. Seth, urged by his mother to commit a murder, finally does so (after the above conversation), but with the most paltry motivation that could be imagined:

> *Seth.* The little funk. Sunlight on sparkling water, its
> shade dissolved, reforming, unreal activity where
> others laughed but he blubbed clinging, homesick,
> and undeveloped form. I'll do it. Men point in
> after days. He always was. But wrongly. He
> fought and overcame, a stern self-ruler.

It will be noticed that in the relationship between Seth and his mother we have almost the same drama of oedipus-complex that exists between Ransome and his mother in 'The Ascent of F. 6' and which lured him to his death. And Seth's motive in committing his crime seems very like Ransome's, the belief that in so doing he will be able to wipe away all the cowardice and weakness of his childhood. But more than that, there is the crux: 'Men point in after days'. The Auden hero is a self-conscious 'twirp', whose main preoccupation is what other people will think. The murder, then, is not only due to a need for psychological readjustment inside Seth, but also balm to his vanity. It will be noticed that a similar type of person is the subject of that admirable poem 'Since you are going to begin to-day | Let us consider what it is you do. | You are the one whose part it is to lean ' | etc. ('Poems', III). This leads me to think (and I hope it is the case) that Auden's treatment of Seth and his friends is satirically and not heroically intended. But however it is intended, that does not alter the fact that Pacifism is the most positive, and the only consistent, political attitude in Auden's poetry, right from that charade to his last book, 'New Year Letter'.

To analyse Auden's work thoroughly in this manner would need a whole book on the subject, but the main outlines of his social outlook are very easily followed. In the 1930 poems the main realization was of a decayed and outworn social system. Many of those poems are little more than catalogues, in which observations of that decay are set down as he sees them in the distressed areas, moving pictures of industrial and rural rot, nightmare landscapes, idle hands:

> I've come a very long way to prove
> No land, no water, and no love.   (IX)

Who stands, the crux left of the watershed
On the wet road between the chafing grass
Below him sees dismantled washing-floors,
Snatches of tramlines running to the wood,
And industry already comatose
Yet sparsely living.   (XI)

Squeeze into the works through broken windows or
     through damp-sprung doors;
See the rotted shafting, see holes gaping in the upper
    floors.   (XXII)

And it is also noticeable that although this book contains
some of the most delicate lyrics Auden has ever written,
his social pessimism penetrates even into his treatment
of human love, for the love poems also have this constant
negative note:

This gratitude for gifts is less
Than the old loss. . . .   (XVIII)

What's in your mind, my dove, my coney,
Do thoughts grow like feathers, the dead end of life;
Is it making of love or counting of money,
O raid on the jewels, the plans of a thief?   (XIII)

It will do murder or betray
For either party equally . . .   (XIV)

(Love) Designs his own unhappiness
    Foretells his own death and is faithless.   (X)

It is, in other words, convincing evidence of the sincerity
and homogeneity of Auden's first book that this element
of pain and frustration runs like a common thread through
the psychological and social interpretations of all the
poems.   Auden began with a defeat-complex which he
has never outgrown.

'The Orators', beneath its boisterous exterior, is also
a sad and disturbing book, though it was a work which
raised temporarily the hopes of those who saw in Auden

an English Mayakovsky. Reading the book with an
adult mind, it is hard to swallow so much bad taste
embedded in so much fine perception and delicate understanding. The book is not much more than a development of a line suggested in what was the worst of the
1930 poems; that which begins:

> We made all possible preparations,
> Drew up a list of firms.   (XII)

In spite of some excellent prose, it was mainly bad
propaganda, deliberate 'writing down' such as discredits
in advance the attempts of 'intellectuals' to take up any
ideological battle.   The plays were a more successful
attempt at raising the social issue to a mythological plane.
It will be noticed, however, that the psychological
apparatus of the plays continually overshadows the
'political' element, and one is tempted to believe that
the more directly political parts were suggested or even
written by Isherwood.   I shall reserve my main conclusions about these plays for a study of modern drama.
It is sufficient to remark that such a device as disguising
Francis as a dog in 'The Dog Beneath the Skin' would,
according to Bergson, preclude any possibility of such
a play rising above the level of farce.   It is this fact
which allowed the bankers, capitalists and aristocrats to
go and see the play and have a good laugh, without in
any way being moved or amazed by the axe that was
being ground.   Many middle-class elements failed to
understand or realize the social implications of the play:
intended to appeal on two levels, very often it only
appealed on one.   In 'The Ascent of F. 6', in the same
way, the political content was completely swamped by
the psychological play with oedipus-complexes and the
whole problem of adolescent mountaineering.   This is
a crude way of putting it.   Far from underestimating

Auden's ability as a playwright, I would say that Auden is the only young writer today who has the makings of a first-class dramatist. He has started at the right end, concentrating on full entertainment value, and adapting the theatre to the inventions of the film. He might even become the great dramatist of the masses, unless this war damps his imagination and wit. But in those early plays it was plain that he was trying to do too much at once, and that as a result the serious part of his work was submerged. That suggests that perhaps the serious part was not sufficiently urgent for Auden himself, that he was himself less interested in it than some have supposed. Remember those lines in 'Spain' about the 'Flat ephemeral pamphlet and the boring meeting'.

In the collection 'Look, Stranger' Auden was much matured and developed. It was here that his 'psychic geography' showed to its fullest advantage. At the same time he was moving from narrow doctrine into a broad sense of community, the tone of his writing becoming more positive than before:

> These moods give no permission to be idle,
> For men are changed by what they do;
> And through loss and anger the hands of the unlucky
> Love one another. . . .

Menacing, but it will be noticed that the menace is still presented in negative terms ('loss', 'unlucky', etc.). The main point was this doctrine of love, culminating in his poem 'Spain', and in the least political of Auden's books, 'Another Time'.

The 'New Year Letter' is sometimes at variance with his previous writing, but the main point is well made:

> Upon each English conscience lie
> Two decades of hypocrisy
> And not a German can be proud
> Of what his apathy allowed. . .

For ten years Auden had warned, and this long poem is naturally a rather wistful but assertive 'I told you so'. This fact is a part-justification for his decision to stay out of the struggle.   There are, however, some signs of tergiversation in his new conception of art and society:

> Art is not life and cannot be
> A midwife to society,
> For art is a fait accompli.

Apart from this unpleasant instance of Auden's latest fad—his rhyming with terms like 'fait accompli', 'solificatio', 'en clair', this pidgin English with its tags of French, German, Latin, Italian and what not—it is depressing to find Auden passing into a reactionary (defeatist) camp of art for art's sake as he is now doing. He writes in a long note: 'Both their unique position in society and the unique nature of their work conspire to make artists less fitted for political thinking than most people.   As citizens they are the *only* people for whom a capitalist democracy is a completely open society. . . .' (He might have added, apart from the bankers, financiers, factory-owners and aristocrats.)   It is pathetic, even though one might agree (as I do) about the writers' incompetence as politicians, to find Auden muddling all his values and talking for a page about 'successful' and 'unsuccessful' intellectuals, or to find him writing: 'Now just as the artist, qua citizen, is the only person for whom society is really open, so, qua artist, i.e. in relation to what he does, he is the only person who is really a dictator.'   Through this salad of 'qua's' and 'i.e.'s' the fact emerges that Auden is flying in the face of fact, forgetting how such writers as Lawrence and Joyce were treated by this society which allows them to be 'dictators'. But dictators of what? 'Tyrants of words and syllables' perhaps, but nothing more serious.   It is true that democracy leaves a great deal of scope and liberty to the writer, perhaps as much as can be expected under any régime, and more than either Fascism (certainly) and Communism (probably) has allowed. But we also know that democracy is a 'free and open society' only to those who are prepared to accept the capitalist premisses, only to those who are prepared, like Bernard Shaw and Wells, to get rich and then move freely. The most surprising thing is that Auden should talk so complacently of 'capitalist democracy'. Is there not such a possibility, not so remote, as a socialist democracy, in which we could expect the writer to have as much liberty as other citizens, but not more? Is there any reason why the writer should profit from privilege while seeing so many of his public excluded from it?

But what about Auden and America? It is, of course, his own business from the point of view of his private life. From the point of view of poetry, the test is whether it has done him any harm as a poet. He had, as I have pointed out, a fairly consistent pacifist attitude before the war: his wife was German; he had already on a hundred occasions protested against the rottenness of Europe. Added to this some disappointment over the German-Russian alliance, and he has every reason for going to America and staying there. But this does not alter the fact that he has not published a good poem since. The reason, I think, is partly that in going to America his verse has lost one of its most solid qualities: it was that his poetry was profoundly English. There was hardly a poem in which his strong sentimental feeling for England did not find expression. In losing contact with England, Auden is likely to lose the most fundamental thing that helped him as a poet. Not seeing England at war will prevent him from ever understanding England again; to have refused to share this suffering, and this silent revolution of feeling which is being accomplished, will mean that he will return here as a stranger. He admits movingly in his 'New Year Letter' all that England meant for him:

> England to me is my own tongue
> And what I did when I was young.
> If now, two aliens in New York,
> We meet, Elizabeth, and talk
> Of friends who suffer in the torn
> Old Europe where we both were born,
> What this refutes or that confirms,
> I can but think and talk in terms
> Of images that I have seen,
> And England tells me what we mean.

But it is evident from this long poem that Auden has failed to understand what has been happening in England in the last two years. He treats the war only as a 'problem', as 'what refutes and what confirms', and has lost all hold of feeling. His imaginative sympathy fails him badly when he can write:

> Thus, squalid beery Burton stands
> For shoddy thinking of all brands,
> The wreck of Rhondda for the mess
> We make when for a short success
> We split our symmetry of art,
> Deny the reason of the Heart. . . .

Really, it is too bad when 'the wreck of Rhondda', with the upheaval in the life of thousands, the death of mothers and children, means little more than occasion for a glib reference to English muddle-headedness and a semi-quotation from Pascal, or a rhyme between mess and success. I cannot see Auden developing in America, and unless he can find a stable outlook to replace his lost Communism he is going to drown himself in this muddle of Pascal, Wagner, Nietzsche, Kierkegaard and a hundred others who provide the stuffing for his notes.

Apart from this, Auden's politics are now being tinged with mysticism and he is moving into something which is a cross between Anarchism and Middleton Murry:

> And all that we can always say
> Is: true democracy begins
> With free confession of our sins;
> And all true unity commences
> In consciousness of differences,
> That all have wants to satisfy
> And each a power to supply . . .

This writing is flat, but with a poet like Auden it is important to remember that there might be such periods of lame writing which indicate a pause before a greater advance. I think that Auden is about to enter, as it were, into Wordsworth's later depressing phase from the point of view of politics. But he might move out of this temporary prosiness and platitude into a firmer and purer way of writing than he had achieved before. Auden himself seems keenly aware of this:

> For I relapse into my crimes;
> Time and again have slubbered through
> With slip and slapdash what I do,
> Adopted what I would disown,
> The preacher's loose immodest tone . . .

IV. *The Style which is no Style*

This essay is already too long to allow of any satisfactory analysis of Auden's technique, if that were necessary. But it is not really necessary, as some of the main points have already been touched, especially the negative ones. The main question now is, why has Auden had such a penetrating influence on the younger writers? A painter recently said to me: 'If I can paint a circle and two splashes of red, and regard my work as

complete, I owe that to Picasso.' The same applies to
Auden: he has been a liberating influence who gave the
younger writers a self-confidence which they might otherwise have had to fight for dearly. Auden broadened into
a highway the path which had been hewn into convention
and hypocrisy by Eliot, Pound, Owen and the vers-
libristes. But he did more. The preceding generation
(those now in their fifties) was composed largely of
intellectual poets—Eliot, Pound, Graves, Riding, Read,
the Sitwells—and it is Auden who broke down the new
snobbery of intellectualism which was in danger of
creating a minority-poetry. He also enlarged, quite
definitely, the poetry-reading public. The most sug-
gestible of poets we have had for a long time, he was
able to synthesize in his work an enormous amount of
the achievements and methods of past writers. Reacting
to numerous influences, he was able to enlarge for younger
writers the vocabulary, syntax, rhythm and imagery of
poetry. That is why so many of the younger poets are
accused of 'deriving' from Auden, when it is not the case.
Most often they have only observed his methods and have
used them in their own way. The truth is that, in a
sense, Auden has done all this at his own expense, almost
to his own detriment. What has happened is that he
has not created his own recognizable manner, as Eliot
did. He has created the 'style which is no style', and in
the 1930 poems alone one could pick out works which
might have been written by such poets as Graves, Owen
and Eliot. Auden has a host of manners, good and bad.
I do not propose to examine them: the pretentious but
effective telegraphese of the 'Paid on Both Sides' which
passes into the impressionist manner of some of his poems;
his 'ciné-style' which is a circular view, as the French
say, of a whole landscape, town or country in a few lines;
that style which is artificially tough and resembles

Hemingway; another style in which he heaps up a series of abstractions, culminating in some of his American poems which, with their personified passions, suggest that this writer is lapsing into the eighteenth century and forgetting what passion is; those obvious devices, internal rhyme, half-rhyme, assonance, sprung-rhythm, the omission of pronouns, verbs and other desirable parts of speech, his puns, his conceits, his incorrect and slipshod epithets which startle momentarily, and all types of slang and private jargon: most of these things have already been adequately reviewed by other critics. It is not the presence of these things which creates the particular climate of Auden's poetry; it is rather the co-existence of them. Eliot, for instance, is always very careful to separate his styles: he passes from one to another, but never confuses them. Any one poem of Auden is likely to be as much a mixed bag as any one of his books, and his books, in their strange juxtaposition of subject and tone, are rather like a cinema crowd emerging, from the stalls, the boxes and the pit, in a confused and democratic mass through the same exit. Sooner or later he will realize this, but if he diminishes this shock which his poems invariably give, he might also kill one of their main charms. Eliot, already so unclassical by the purest standards, is as champagne to a cocktail when compared with Auden.

What are the real qualities of Auden? One of them is certainly an imaginative interest in the way people live. Even when he misinterprets, as in the case of Honeyman, he is not far wrong in his background. It is this which gives him great potentialities as a popular poet. And this interest and sympathy do not fail him when he moves from miners, shopkeepers and little bourgeois to consider the minds of Yeats and Freud. And he has also a realization of the vastness and one-ness of the human scene. We have seen already that he has no one-track mind: he does not see Spain as an isolated phenomenon, but as a symbol of the consciousness of the world, and he usually treats any subject, however small, in its broadest implications. This also fits him for the part of popular poet. Thirdly, his naïveness, in spite of his sometimes heartless jibes and his intellectual leg-pulling, has remained unspoiled, and he is capable of expressing a primitive and pure feeling, as in such poems as 'O lay your sleeping head, my love' or his now famous 'Madrigal'. That this is still alive in him is seen in the best parts of the 'New Year Letter'.

Fourthly, Auden has also that vast, living vocabulary which is essential to any poet who wants to be of his time and of the future. He is enabled by this to write on many levels. He is also sensitive (much more than many who have followed him) to the musical qualities of words, though he has shown a tendency to fall rhythmically into rather set patterns, that of such lines as

> The sensitive amusers
> And masked amazers,

or 'August for the people and their favourite islands'; that is to say, types of rhythm which run with an easy lilt and usually end with this light syllable, or a dying fall.

The most important point about Auden's style is that, for good or ill, he has tried to write a poetry very close to common speech, and that he has succeeded. Generally speaking, one might say that in his early poems he tried to express a fairly universal, and in any case a second-hand, subject-matter in an intensely personal style, and since then he has moved towards a more personal subject-matter and a more impersonal style. His ideas are being more and more imprinted with his own particular twist of mind, and one sees increasingly that he is quite

B

incapable of orthodoxy of any kind. Whether Auden once more moves towards a more richly personal idiom, to replace the rather threadbare idiom, full of foreign clichés, which he has recently been using, is his own business, but it is quite certain, in comparing his poems written in 1939 with those written in 1940 and 1941, that Auden is not yet a hardened and stabilized poet. That is, Auden is still in full development and undergoing a similar crisis to Eliot's after 'The Waste Land'.

July-August 1941.

STEPHEN SPENDER: A SENSITIVE

I. *Isolation*

THOUGH Spender has been fairly sanely criticized by his contemporaries, he has rarely been considered on his own merits, and too often merely in relation to the group of poets with which he is associated. As he seems to me to differ from Auden, Lewis and Macneice much more than he resembles them, some clarification is necessary.

There is a basis of acceptance of a social outlook in Auden and Lewis which is much stronger in them than in Spender. Spender has his own drama: a struggle to adapt his individualism to his social views, and a struggle to understand and perfect his individuality. Those who sneer at Spender's introspection are those who have never understood Wordsworth or Eliot, Shelley or Baudelaire.

Another difference, and it goes so far as to become a radical defect, is that Spender in his poetry describes almost entirely things he does not like, including himself. Such things are time, fear, war, death, inhibition, weakness. This proclaims him a critical poet, a moralist, as almost any self-conscious poet is bound to become. But there are moments of powerful lyrical flight in his poems which indicate that he will develop into a primarily lyrical poet.

Considering poetry as human gesture, the logical result of Spender's description of dislikes is that his typical rhythms are those of hesitation and recoil, a dropping of hands. This determines also his syntax, and the final result is quite unlike the writing of his friends. To take examples, here are three of his ways of grammatical-rhythmic expression:

(*a*) A breaking of the poem into minute units, creating a slow rhythm corresponding to effort of thought:

> (1) Different living | is not living | in different places |
> But creating | in the mind | a map |
> Creating | in the mind | a desert | ('Poems', 1933)

> (2) If I could | accept
> Myself | in those | in whose
> Sweetness | my life dissolves |
> And trust they could accept |
> Themselves | in me; | nor fear |
> ('The Still Centre', 1939)

(*b*) Delayed action:

> Only this rose |
> My friend laid on my breast, | and these few lines |
> Written from home, | *are real*.   ('Poems', 1933)

(*c*) Inversion, which also produces a reluctant rhythm:

> Now cloudy peaks are bared; the Mystic One
> Horizons haze, as the blue incense heaven.
> Peace, peace. . . . Then splitting skull and dream, there comes
> Blotting out lights, the trumpeter, the sun.

Actually in this last extract these three methods are seen very effectively combined. This deliberation and slowness explain why Spender is the least accessible of the younger poets: he seems chary of opening his hands and offering anything. His poems are as hard to read as they probably were to write. The fact that Spender has avoided fixed forms does not mean he is lazy: on the contrary, his discipline is in the placing of words, not in the placing of stress or rhyme. These things, which correspond to a psychological necessity, define the texture of his poetry. It is intricately interwoven, full of nuances and refinements like Eliot's, and eminently personal. In this he differs extremely from Auden (save in some of

STEPHEN SPENDER

Auden's 1930 poems). Auden's texture is at once looser
and coarser, less subtle and more masculinely direct.
Macneice's texture, compared with Spender's, is so easy
and fluid, sleek and correct, as to appear machine-made.
For Macneice still relies on all the traditional rules and
regulations which Spender has discarded.

II. *The Wilfred Owen of the Peace*

Auden is obviously a poet who thrives best when he
feels he has a message and a mission, but there is every
sign that Spender, who has also had a message, would
be much happier without one. He seems, from the start,
to have had politics thrust upon him, partly by the
Liberal atmosphere in which he was reared. Not that
this was particularly distasteful to him, for he wrote in
a number of 'New Verse' in 1937: 'I was always
interested in politics. . . . I think he (Auden) disapproved
of my politics, just as, at that time, he disapproved of my
writing prose or going to concerts to hear classical
music.' But it is one thing being interested in politics,
and another trying to reconcile Communism and
Individualism in poetry.

Spender's social attitude seems clear enough, though
it has been very scathingly treated in some quarters. He
was once described by someone as 'The Rupert Brooke
of the depression'. But the joke—which is a bad one
in any case, since one poet's name should not be used to
beat another—the joke can be turned, and the half-truth
completed, by calling him the Wilfred Owen of the peace.
That would not be adequate to represent his attitude,
which has been very different from the sheep-like
acceptance of Brooke and the clamorous, pitiful protest
of Owen. Spender has tried to be far more than a
negation: during the depression he was not merely

depressed, but explored the possibilities of a social doctrine and tried to integrate it into poetry.

An instance of the type of injustice to which I refer is to be found in an article by Mr Randall Swingler in 'Our Time' in May 1941. Writing of Auden, Spender, Macneice and Lewis, he declared: 'Their literature was a literature of adolescence, precocious in technique, absorbed by the problem of the individual ego's position in the world, clothed in its own extravagant fantasy, full of gigantic hopes, impatient dreams and a belief in the miraculous.' Mr Swingler has not reached the root of the problem. It can, indeed, be replied that this adolescent, precocious literature mightily stirred the youth of the 'thirties, and turned many young men towards the Left who might easily have become Fascists had that influence been lacking. And it was precisely that power of treating political theory as a myth, an adventure, which was the most precious quality of the work of Auden, Spender and Lewis. No political or social doctrine can make much headway in the minds of a people unless it is constantly reinfused with passion and imagination. Engels understood this quite well when he wrote: 'Generally speaking, the poetry of past revolutions (always excepting the Marseillaise) rarely exerts a revolutionary influence in later times, because, to act upon the masses, it must also reflect the momentary prejudices of the people.' (Letter to Schlüter, 1885.)

But Mr Swingler goes farther, writing: 'When they became "revolutionary" it was in order to revolutionize literature, not society.' Are we to believe, then, that Auden and his friends deliberately isolated themselves from their own class for the fun of the thing, and for ten years packed their voluminous work with revolutionary ideas in which they did not believe? I think Mr Swingler is using very naïve measures to dispose of these writers who have tried to show that individualism, contrary to the notions of those 'Communists' who have destroyed Communism, *is* compatible with liberty and equality. Marx, I think, would have disapproved of Mr Swingler. Arnold's inscription on the tombstone of Shelley's ideals no longer makes us smile. What did Marx think of Shelley? He said: 'The real difference between Byron and Shelley lies in this: those who understand and love them consider it fortunate that Byron died at the age of thirty-six, for he would have become a bourgeois reactionary had he lived much longer; they regret, on the contrary, that Shelley died at twenty-nine, for he was entirely revolutionary and would always have belonged to the vanguard of Socialism' (Ed. Aveling and Eleonore Marx-Aveling: 'Shelley Sozialist' in 'Die Neue Zeit', 1888, p. 541). It is true that Marx's taste in literature was far from infallible, but, like all great sociologists—Comte is another instance—so far from despising poets, he read them with great care and sympathy and seemed to understand that the poet can give a quintessence of human aspirations. For it is only by writing what is nearest his heart that a writer can be effective in helping to revolutionize society. *His first job is to revolutionize literature.*

The accusation of insincerity and futility directed against Spender (who stands, incidentally, very much in the same relation to Auden as Shelley did to Byron) is very wide of the mark. The critics in political blinkers should realize that these poets of the 'thirties, producing works like Spender's 'Vienna', Auden's 'Spain', Barker's 'Calamiterror' and Day Lewis's 'The Nabara', represent first of all a disintegration of the bourgeoisie, and secondly a disintegration of bourgeois aesthetic values. A discussion of their 'sincerity', besides being impertinent, is a waste of time unless these two facts are recognized.

III. *The Struggle*

Psychology and politics are so interdependent, however, that it might not be amiss to examine some of Spender's political poems more closely. This much must be conceded to Mr Swingler, that Spender is too subtle and complicated to express himself in black and white, or in the rigmarole of the Communist Manifesto.

The atmosphere of his poems is one of struggle. This is seen even in such of his poems as seem to me most 'positive'. There is, for instance, the 'Oh young men, oh young comrades' in the 'Poems':

> Oh young men, oh young comrades,
> It is too late now to stay in those houses
> Your fathers built where they built you to build to breed
> Money on money. It is too late
> To make or even to count what has been made.

Very much the Auden of the 1930 poems ('If we really want to live, we'd better start at once to try', etc.), but with a difference, that world of difference between passionate and theoretical propaganda. The tone of these lines, and of the whole poem, is characteristic of Spender: though quiet and intimate, it is none the less forceful. Surely this is a legitimate way of persuasion, as convincing as anything that can be said in Hyde Park or 'Our Time'; and the subsequent urge, 'advance to rebuild . . . advance to rebel', throws a new light on this 'precocious adolescent' poet. But he continues:

> Count rather those fabulous possessions
> Which begin with your body and your fiery soul;
> The hairs on your head, the muscles extending
> In ranges with their lakes across your limbs.
> Count your eyes as jewels and your valued sex,
> Then count the sun and the innumerable coined light.
> Sparkling on waves and spangling under trees.

This sensual element in Spender is fundamental, and compensates fully for a certain lack of humour and the lack of broad historical and geographical views, subtlety of reference, and all those other advantages which help the poems of Auden and Macneice to shine glossily at first sight. But nothing, in any poet, can compensate for a lack of sensual understanding, which we usually call imagination, and which is to be found in abundance in Spender's poems. This last statement needs qualification: that is to say, which appears in most of Spender's poems but is rarely sustained. In this particular poem (as in many others of his political poems) it makes the politics more acceptable: but it might well be that the lyrical flights in Spender's propagandist poems occur largely as reactions against what he is preaching. I have used, almost by accident, the word 'compensate': I might now go so far as to say that when Spender goes into the difficult details of an ideology he escapes at times into sensual imagery in the Freudian sense of the term 'compensation'. . . . Be that as it may, the above quotation seems to me to illustrate the best of Spender. It is useless to object, as Macneice and John Lehmann have done, that Spender sometimes falls into 'over-prettiness' in his imagery: no image is 'over-pretty' when it is emotionally exact and apt to its context. Such words as those used here—'fabulous', 'fiery', 'jewels', 'sparkling' and 'spangling'—are, theoretically, of the type of words which, according to Dr I. A. Richards, evoke what are called 'stock-responses'; labour-savers which mean a short-cut to the reader's appreciation. Is this so bad as it has been painted? During the 'thirties, poets were thumped into obedience by a number of critics, chiefly professors, editors of small reviews and journalists, who in their intellectual snobbery set out to restrict the vocabulary of poetry; a set of miniature Malherbes and

Doctor Johnsons, 'tyrants of words and syllables'.
Beware any ill-advised poet who dared use such words
as 'love', 'rose', 'silver' or 'golden'! As a reaction
against an overworked 'poetic' vocabulary this was very
wholesome and necessary, and it certainly infused new
energy into the poetry of the younger generation. But
it is with the greatest caution that such temporary purges
should be given high-sounding names and set up as
golden rules. The whole problem of the 'stock-response'
surely resides in context. The words 'I love you' are
perhaps the most overworked in any language, but that
does not deprive them of their value, which depends
solely on how and when they are used. There is one
thing, however, which I notice in Spender's use of such
words: it is that one feels the emotional impact of his
poems before the intellectual impact. This is a somewhat
disturbing aspect of much of modern poetry; but not
peculiar to the younger generation: I found myself
similarly affected by Eliot's 'Ash Wednesday' and
Pound's 'Cantos' before I appreciated fully their intellectual implications. The fact that this also happens in
reading such highly concentrated poets as Donne and
Racine, in whom, none the less, the intellectual argument
would seem to be very urgent, leads me to suspect that
poetry of any value must appeal first, and perhaps
above all, to the emotions. And perhaps it is because of
this, and not because of the mysterious 'suspension of
disbelief' of which Dr Richards has made so much, that
a Protestant can obtain immediate pleasure from the
writing of an atheist or a Catholic. The history of man
shows us that for practical purposes 'suspension of disbelief' is *at any time* a highly unlikely procedure: it is
more to the point to urge that, when confronted with
real poetry, our emotions are *moved whether we want to
be moved or not*, and we read on, not in order to be con-

vinced, but in order to sustain the feeling of pleasure which has been stimulated.

There is another 'political' poem in Spender's first collection which is worth closer inspection; 'Not palaces, an era's crown', which might well bear the title 'Programme'. Typically enough, there is the usual brilliant patch of spontaneity in the middle of the poem, beginning:

> Eye, gazelle, delicate wanderer,
> Drinker of horizon's fluid line. . . .

The essentials of the 'programme' are simple. 'It is too late for rare accumulation' and all the bourgeois habits. But (as is very noticeable, side by side with the cult of defeat and weakness) the poet suddenly develops an almost Nietzschean cult of energy and will:

> I say, stamping the words with emphasis,
> Drink from here energy and only energy
> As from the electric charge of a battery,
> To will this Time's change. . . .

There follows, as in the previous poem quoted, a new appeal for a sensuous appreciation of life, and Spender's recipe for the breakdown of inhibition is seen complete in one poem. The 'Marxist', I suppose, will at once smile and say 'Escapism', but that is just where he will be wrong. Modern psychology has, since Marx, progressed far enough to assure us that the liberation of man must be, simultaneously, internal as well as external. Spender realizes this, and his programme is complete:

> No spirit here seek rest. But this: No man
> Shall hunger: Man shall spend equally.
> Our goal which we compel: Man shall be man.

The poem ends with a condemnation of war and oppression. Now this poem might not seem worth detailed attention. The three lines quoted above, indeed, are aesthetically unsatisfying, and their very roundabout grammatical structure, containing suppressions and inversions which convey an artificial 'toughness', is typical of the vices not only of Spender but of Auden also. But the poem shows the limits to which the alliance between poetry and politics can safely go. The poet cannot afford to present more than the cream, the essence, the idealism of a political outlook. And it becomes obvious that, bound to universal and not local truths, there is little hope for the poet outside a general humanitarian outlook. The poet, concerned with human values, betrays humanity when he descends to the values of a caste or class. All these things for which Spender clamours in this poem might be found in the nineteenth-century Utopists and Liberals. The truth is, that Spender *is* a Liberal. But they are the only values which survive all the vagaries and hatreds of party politics, and there was never greater need for their reaffirmation than the present time.

IV. '*Le Culte du Moi*'

Spender's long poem, 'Vienna', was not very successful, and again demonstrated that his outlook was too broad to allow of any 'party-line' in his poetry. The same can be said of the poems he wrote during the Spanish Civil War. In his Preface to 'The Still Centre', Spender wrote: 'As I have decidedly supported one side—the Republican—in that conflict, perhaps I should explain why I do not strike a more heroic note. My reason is that a poet can only write about what is true to his own experience. . . . Poetry does not state truth, it states the conditions within which something *felt* is true.' His Spanish poems are definitely defeatist. First of all, because he proves himself incapable of the hatred and

animosity such as righteous indignation might evoke—
and which, indeed, are not lacking in the 'Flowering
Rifle' of Roy Campbell whose sympathies were on the
other side of the barricade.   Secondly, because he says
nothing of the generous instincts of the people, the
vitality of their idealism, which was the only bright side
of that war.   Instead of these things he strikes an elegiac,
and sometimes ironic note, lamenting the squandering
of youth and idealism in death.   All this is in keeping
with the humanitarian pacifism of the 'programme'
poem.

Spender's attitude to death is a faithful reflection of
his attitude to life.   In 'Thoughts During an Air Raid'
(a failure as a poem, since Spender is quite incapable of
irony) he writes:

> The essential is
> That all the I's should remain separate
> Propped up under flowers, and no one suffer
> For his neighbour.

Spender saw the war from the point of view of each
individual, not from that of an entire community
struggling for its life.   This individual feeling is even
projected on to a vaster plane—one of which Owen
would have been incapable—when he writes of two
armies at night:

> a common suffering
> Whitens the air with breath and makes both one
> As though these enemies slept in each other's arms.

In time of war, men have a tendency to lose sight of the
individual, and to forget, in their enthusiasm, that man
is not yet so advanced towards freedom that he can be
considered more important than an idea or a circumstance.   For the Nazi and, I regret to say, the Communist,
little or no thought can be given to the value of a human

life, and at the present time the democracies, with their casual lists of slaughtered women and children, are becoming equally indifferent. The so-called 'heroic' conception of war as willing self-sacrifice is only another disguise for a primitive callousness to this greatest of all human values, life. I prefer Spender's quiet realization of the complexity of the problem—the grandeur of man, opposed to his insignificance in a semi-conscious society—to all the heroic poems produced during the Spanish war or this one:

> I gather all my life and pour
> Out its love and comfort here.
> To populate his loneliness,
> And to bring his ghost release,
> My love and pity shall not cease
> For a lifetime at least.

With the Spanish war, Spender's growing awareness of individual life led him, I think, towards a solution of his own personal problem. There is no space to show that development here, but the reader will find it clearly exposed in the poems 'The Uncreating Chaos' (in which, after enumerating his fears, it is obvious that he suggests the traditional anarchist's escape from himself into love), 'Darkness and Light' (the same theme allegorically treated in terms of birth), and finally in 'The Human Situation' and 'Variations on my Life'. 'The Human Situation' is a crucial point in Spender's development, not because it marks anything new, but because it is a summary of his past statements on the individual. This poem is in some respects a catalogue of fears and enemies, reinforced by a certain pride of self:

> And if this I were destroyed,
> The image shattered,
> My perceived, rent world would fly
> In an explosion of final judgement

> To the ends of the sky,
> The colour in the iris of the eye.

But he ends with the logical acceptance of self, the very solution which was forced upon such writers as Nietzsche and Gide, the realization that their weakness is their strength:

> Here I am forced on to my knees,
> On to my real and own and only being
> As into the fortress of my final weakness.

There is no advance on this in 'Variations on my Life', which is again largely nostalgic, but the poem might be read as a means of seeing how the personal problem can be treated in a purely objective way. The finger of Eliot is traceable in the technique of this poem. But the main point about these personal poems is that they are very unlike anything we have in English. I think that Spender is more like Rilke, who shared the same humiliations, and who sought similar compensations. I think Rilke might have written about Napoleon, for instance, very much as Spender did in 'Napoleon in 1814'. The 'Napoleon' presented there is not at all true to the facts, but an immense Spender, with all the complexes and defeatisms a thousand times magnified. This also shows the limitations of Spender, while showing that those limitations might develop, as they did in Rilke, into powers. While his range of interests seems limited, so that his poetry represents a very minute field of vision, his sight, insight, imagery and rhythm are intensely personal. It is this fundamental *reliance upon his own powers*—which quite contradicts all his theories of personal weakness—which marks him as a poet who has been building solidly and might develop beyond those of his contemporaries who developed quickly but depended too much on external stimuli.

V. *Sensibility*

It is impossible, though, to judge a poet merely by his attitudes and his doctrine, for at best the critic who does so must fall into what Baudelaire called 'The heresy of teaching', or what Day Lewis meant when he wrote: 'It is always dangerous and impertinent to commend a poem for anything but its poetry.'

It has already been noticed that Spender's rhythms coincide very well psychologically with his inhibitions. It goes without saying that at times, when his restraint loosens, the rhythm also loosens, and at such moments Spender attains his fullest power. But even that does not change the fact that, fundamentally, there is something unpleasant about his poems. This is no insult, for I find Rimbaud equally unpleasant. The unpleasantness might be partly due to the occasionally cramped gesture of the rhythms, but I think it springs more frequently from the violence and cruelty of his imagery. This violent imagery is very frequently sadistic, disquietingly so. Here are a few instances from different poems:

> I laugh because my laughter
> Is like justice, twisted by a howitzer.
>
> Our eyes mud these scraps rub on.
>
> Heads bounce down stone steps
>
> Hands severed from the wrists
> Moving only with the thoughts in fingers.

Viewed dispassionately, such lines represent fairly well one of those general merits of modern poetry, better seen in lines which are less bloodthirsty, but which show the same contracting, compressing gesture, as opposed to a gesture of expansion and dilution:

And the watching of cripples pass
With limbs shaped like questions.

Time
Monstrous with stillness like the Himalayan range.

Only the world changes, and Time its tense.

But compression does not always mean, as it does here,
a certain unwillingness to expand, and in some poets an
inability to sustain observation. At the risk of making
what might look like a catalogue of different aspects of
Spender, here are a few instances of concentrated but sustained writing, which come as rewards after reading many
a poem by the same author which seems inarticulate and
barren:

Summer struck
Water over rocks, and half the world
Became a ship with a deep keel, the booming floes
And icebergs with their little birds. . . .

('Polar Expedition.' On the whole a homosexual poem,
much Eliot and Auden in it, but well constructed and the
verbal harmonies full and sonorous.)

And
In the green meadows, girls in their first
Summer dresses play. The hurdy-gurdy noise
Trumpets the valley, while egg-freckled arms
Weave their game. Children gather
Pap-smelling cowslips. Papers
Weightless as clouds, browse on the hills.

('Easter Monday.' Spender says he wrote this poem,
and others in the same section, with 'considerable elaboration'. The poems in this first part of 'The Still Centre'
should set Spender a standard for his future lyrical writing.
Strange to say, he writes more lyrically when dealing with
what he calls 'subjects', and about children and other real
people, than when he writes his nostalgias and political
views.)

Break, O break open, till they break the town
And show the children to the fields and all their world

Azure on their sands, to let their tongues
Run naked into books, the white and green leaves open
The history theirs whose language is the sun.

('An Elementary School Class Room in a Slum.' The
same sensual urge as in the praise of youth in an earlier
poem quoted above. Good coincidence of free rhythm
and thought here. A good instance of Spender's Rous-
seauistic conception of childhood.)

On the chalk cliff edge struggles the final field
Of barley smutted with tares and marbled
With veins of rusted poppy as though the plough had
bled.
The sun is drowned in bird-wailing mist,
The sea and sky meet outside distinction,
The landscape glares and stares—white poverty
Of gaslight diffused through frosted glass.

('The Marginal Field.' This is an instance of another,
less sentimental type of description. General effect good,
but weak points obvious on close analysis. First three lines
a perfect rhythmic and sense-unity. The rest of the
description incidental and superfluous. Line four: concentration of double image, 'drowned' and 'bird-wailing'
(an invisible crying of birds through mist), unsuccessful,
because violence of first image and feebleness of second in
contrast create bathos. Line five—not satisfactory and a
little pedantic in tone—can mean no more, and perhaps
less, than 'out of sight of naked eye'—nothing to do with
the field. 'Glares and stares' obviously for harmony, but
I think this enfeebles verse when the two homophones mean
the same. Last line: the urban image comprehensible,
but I think anti-climax after the brilliant colour and sharp
outline of first three lines. I chose this first verse of poem
instinctively, and realize on analysis that, far from being
'observed', as the first three lines lead one to think, the
landscape is almost entirely emotionally created. This is
not 'wrong', only I think the emotion stronger in the opening, and falsely emotionalized in the rest.)

As a child holds a pet
Arms clutching but with hands that do not join
And the coiled animal watches the gap

To outer freedom in animal air,
So the earth-and-rock flesh arms of this harbour
Embrace but do not enclose the sea
Which, through a gap, vibrates to the open sea
Where ships and dolphins swim and above is the sun.

(From 'Port Bou'. As a whole, this is a more convincing landscape than the above. Why? Because what is extraneous to the 'reporter' description is not induced sentiment, but one closely identified to the object. The image of the child holding a pet corresponds very well to the lay-out of the harbour. The fanciful introduction of dolphins might represent a romantic landlubber's conception of the sea: at the same time it conveys fully the bobbing motion of the ship—a motion also suggested convincingly in the rhythm of the line.

Actually these first few lines do not form a complete unity, so let us consider them in relation to the completed description):

In the bright winter sunlight I sit on the stone parapet
Of a bridge; my circling arms rest on a newspaper
Empty in my mind as the glittering stone
Because I search for an image
And seeing an image I count out the coined words
To remember the childish headlands of the harbour.

(Description of landscape is usually bettered by human presence. Here, a troublesome element is introduced, the vagueness of 'Empty in my mind as the glittering stone'. Though the stone probably refers to the bridge, I find the ambiguity of ' Empty in my mind':=there is empti(ness) in my mind= . . . no, it is not ambiguity but a definite obscurity. But something else is sensed here: the re-creation, in the simple picture of the poet's arms outstretched before him, of the landscape and the child-image. This amounts to the cunning and highly successful trick of the Dutch picture-within-a-picture and, I think, brings out better than anything the fitting reply to those who see Spender as a purely ingenuous poet.)

There is a depth of tenderness in Spender which, as

can be seen from the above extract, or from such lines as

> Children, who extend their smiles of crystal,
> And their leaping gold embrace . . .

gives both depth and power to his descriptions provided that he describes things he likes, things which provoke the deeper levels of his sensibility. 'Ne méprisez la sensibilité de personne', wrote Baudelaire; and I wonder whether contemporary poetry would not be infinitely better than it is, if the modern hard-boiled façade were discarded and people would consent once more to be human. In the age of the machine, in the age when the study of man's life is becoming a 'science' and we are forgetting that life can also be an art, in an age when sensibility is hardened by brutal warfare and the undignified poverties and humiliations of peace, there is more need than ever for a revival of sensibility, even at the risk of disturbing rationalities of outlook which can be good, much as Rousseau did in the eighteenth century. Surrealism, with its own pseudo-science and pseudo-politics, was not the way. And the contrast between Spender's unpleasant political poems and the extracts quoted above suggests that hatred or stimulated pity are not the way. What is needed is the perfect balance between outer and inner reality which Spender has so thoroughly achieved in poems like 'Port Bou' and his poems about children.

June-July 1941.

LOUIS MACNEICE:

POETRY AND COMMON SENSE

As civilization augments and philosophy grows, we commonly find a school of 'common-sense' poets, as they may be called, arise and develop, who proceed to describe what they see around them, to describe its *natura naturans*, to delineate its *natura naturata*, to evolve its productive agencies, to pursue their own subtle ramifications.—WALTER BAGEHOT.

I. *Being Augustan*

BAGEHOT, writing on Pope and Cowper, characterizes in these few words much of the poetry of our own century, when the 'Observer' poets, and many others of the present generation have been more than usually conscious of the social origins and bearing of poetry. Psychology, politics, the latest discoveries of economic theory, images drawn from factory and surgery, have all been assimilated into poetry in this effort of creating work which takes a definite place in its social context. In the case of Shakespeare the plays, on internal evidence, might just as well have been written by an aristocrat, a bourgeois or a struggling player—as well by William Stanley, Earl of Derby, as my friend Mr Macdonald-Lucas has argued in his book on the subject, as by a common actor springing from the people. Today, such doubts about the origins of our poetry are practically impossible, since the poets leave no stone unturned to reveal beyond question their opinions on politics, economics, education and birth-control. What has happened is that poetry is being increasingly confused with opinion, and it is this which brings the poetry of the past twenty years into close contact with that of the Augustan age. It is not surprising that many of the younger poets have spoken highly of Dryden—though the youngest of these speak more frequently of Blake—but it is surprising that, in spite of their admiration, their work has only superficial contact with that of their master. They have none of his urbanity, his poise, his power for hard work which so smooths down every corner that some of his poems might have been written by a machine, or on glass with a diamond; they lack his staying power, and that aristo-cratic violence which enabled him to scourge his opponents without as much as ruffling his wig; they lack that virtuosity which enabled him to write on any subject with distinction; and above all, they lack that firm sense of purpose and defined direction which in Dryden was so marked. It is one thing to borrow a poet's conception of his art, and another to acclimatize it to a vastly changed society and language. Macneice, who in so many ways represents this neo-Dryden school, when he writes of the social virtues of the poet as one who should be a reader of newspapers, interested in economics, interested in women, and able-bodied, produced a different response from Shaftesbury, Chesterfield and many more who have written of the English conception of the gentleman-scholar. For in our times the qualities he mentions are no longer confined to the poet or the gentleman; they are, rather, those qualifications which any young salesman or aspiring journalist is expected by his employers to possess.

It was T. S. Eliot who turned the attention of the young poets towards Dryden, but it is obvious that he understood, much better than most, what can profitably be learnt from that writer. Having absorbed about the only thing which can, at this time, be learnt from Dryden —his sense of balance, his stream-lined elimination of all superfluity—Eliot turned into paths which are not those dictated by a predominantly social theory of poetry. This is borne out by his peculiar development from the

LOUIS MACNEICE

[Photo Elliott & Fry

social and psychological realism of 'Prufrock', 'Portrait of a Lady', 'The Waste Land' and the Sweeney poems, to the 'Pure Poetry'—very much in line with Claudel and Bremond—phase of 'Ash Wednesday' and minor poems of that period, to arrive finally at that masterful, sensual expression of pure thought—which again brings him, vastly changed, to another aspect of Dryden—which is to be found in his latest and richest poems, 'Burnt Norton', 'East Coker' and 'The Dry Salvages', variations on a plain but vital theme. Eliot has purified his poetry, moving from the coarse externals of modern—and therefore incidental—life to the inner realities of life. In other words, he has moved, very logically, from the particular to the general, and his poetry has thereby moved to a less personal level than his earlier work gave reason to suppose. This he has done in direct contrast to the majority of contemporary poets (though perhaps this is the main distinction between the generation now in their fifties and those in their twenties and thirties, since Eliot stands in a clear relationship to Laura Riding, Robert Graves, Herbert Read and Edwin Muir), for while he surveys life in this metaphysical manner, the younger poets are still in their overalls, smelling of their contact with the pub, the factory, the machine, the meeting and all the accidents of everyday life. The point to which we come is this: that an admiration for the Augustans, or a parallel with their conception of poetry, can be diversely interpreted, and where the younger poets are closer in spirit to Pope's occasional rough-and-tumble in the alleys of London, the older poets have drawn closer to that spirit of abstraction which characterizes certain writings of Dryden.

Louis Macneice is a stylist, in the best sense, and one who, by his attempt at grasping the rougher realities of modern life, has on occasion deliberately written in a

loose and carefree manner. A review of one of his books
in 'Scrutiny' appeared biased and unfair, but there was
no denying that the lapses of style of which he was
accused were present. That does not alter the fact that
he can also write with exceptional purity, and that in
the total composition of a poem he has a mature architectural sense. But he is not single-minded, and for that
reason will provide a successor neither to Eliot nor
Dryden. He can be considered a very good representative
of many of the young poets, some of whom appear in
this book, who have failed to make up their mind
about society, philosophy and religion, and whose
tragedy is that they are aimlessly drifting through a
hostile world, and failing to use their talent to the best
advantage.

II. *Poetry and Common Sense*

Macneice showed himself at once in his first book a
pitiless critic of modern society, and it is on this aspect
of his work that we shall dwell for the moment. He
brought an almost exclusively destructive attitude to
modern life, which he set out to analyse in a variety of
ways:

> It is better we should go quickly, go into Asia
> Or any other tunnel where the world recedes,
> Or turn blind wantons like the gulls who scream
> And rip the edge off any ideal or dream.
>
> ('Poems', 1935)

'And rip the edge off any ideal or dream': that is
the function of the analyst, and of the common-sense
school. It is this Stendhalian 'horror of being a dupe'
which dictates all Macneice's subsequent writings on
politics, literature, nature and love. Writing at that
time of Communism, he said:

> But before you proclaim the millennium, my dear,
> Consult the barometer—
> This poise is perfect, but maintained
> For one day only.

In this respect he differs from the Auden group with which he has long been associated; he refuses, like poets younger than himself such as Allott, Symons, Dylan Thomas and Barker, to take any definite stand. But that did not affect his deep awareness of the oncoming destruction of many precious things:

> Our freedom as free lances
> Advances towards the end;
> The Earth compels, upon it
> Sonnets and birds descend;
> And soon, my friend,
> We shall have no time for dances.

This ominous note, 'no time for dances', is one which occurs frequently in Macneice's books, especially in 'Autumn Journal'. The third section of 'Autumn Journal'—in which book, by the way, Macneice broke away from his Gauterian purity of form—is well worth some attention if an analysis of his social attitude (though this is not the best way of approaching a poet) is to be complete.

In this section, Macneice ventures into the social problem of work, and with a certain superior contempt, mingled with pity, contemplates the working man:

> Now the till and the typewriter call the fingers,
>   The workman gathers his tools
> For the eight-hour day, but after that the solace
>   Of films or football pools
> Or of the gossip or cuddle, the moments of self-glory
>   Or self-indulgence. . . .

This contemplation then gives rise to a more positive

declaration which shows where Macneice's true sympathies lie:

> Most are accepters, born and bred to harness,
>   And take things as they come,
> But some refusing harness and more who are refused it
>   Would pray that another and a better Kingdom come,
> Which now is sketched in the air or travestied in slogans
>   Written in chalk or tar on stucco or plaster-board
> But in time may find its body in men's bodies,
>   Its law and order in their heart's accord,
> Where skill will no longer languish nor energy be trammelled
>   To competition and graft. . . .

But it is characteristic of Macneice—who thereby reveals a delicate sensitiveness under his occasionally devil-may-care exterior—that as soon as he approaches something positive he recoils. He suddenly suspects that he, also, has 'the slave-owner's mind', that he also wants 'the skimmings of the cream', and replies that habit has largely made him so:

>   for habit makes me
> Think victory for one implies another's defeat,
> That freedom means the power to order, and that in order
>   To preserve the values dear to the élite
> The élite must remain a few.

This is the common objection of the intellectual and the refined to problems of universal education and universal equality and justice, but Macneice finally refuses this attitude, though not so definitely that he can avoid concluding with no more than a hope that he will have courage to pursue his instinctive belief in the equalities of man:

>   but the worst of all
> Deceits is to murmur 'Lord, I am not worthy',
>   And, lying easy, turn your face to the wall.
> But may I cure that habit, look up and outwards,
>   And may my feet follow my wider glance,
> First no doubt to stumble, then to walk with the others,
>   And in the end—with time and luck—to dance.

It is, then, his intellectual honesty which has kept this poet apart from the impetuous stream of Left poets.

But this hesitation to adopt any preconceived ideology does not rob Macneice of one of his greatest charms, his outspokenness on current affairs, though it gives an unusual colour to his interpretation of them. A good instance of this is his treatment of the Munich affair in 1938 in his 'Autumn Journal'. Already, like George Barker, he foreshadowed the abdication of some of his group from the present war. He saw the Munich crisis, with no surprise, as something for which we had long been waiting and working:

> And at this hour of the day it is no good saying
> > 'Take away this cup';
> Having helped to fill it ourselves, it is only logic
> > That now we should drink it up.

But he goes much farther than this. The irony of this entire section of the poem is subtle, cutting many ways: against the statesmen responsible, against the people, and against himself also, for many of the reactions he satirizes appear to be not far from his own:

> And we who have been brought up to think 'Gallant
> > Belgium'
> > > As so much blague
> Are now preparing again to essay good through evil
> > For the sake of Prague.

And after the Munich agreement between Hitler and Chamberlain:

> The crisis is put off and things look better
> And we feel negotiation is not in vain—
> > Save my skin and damn my conscience. . . .
>
> . . . And stocks go up and wrecks
> Are salved and politicians' reputations
> > Go up like Jack on the Beanstalk; only the Czechs
> > Go down without fighting.

The disgust in this ironic 'we', and the ambiguous last line are fairly balanced by the unmistakable relief which penetrates the passage. But it looks very odd in face of his previous sneering comparison of Czecho-Slovakia with 'Gallant Belgium'. . . .

There is no need to pursue this enquiry farther, having once ascertained that the 'common sense' poet, in such an age as ours, has a very thin time when compared with the Augustans, who lived in a world of more ordered ideas, more calculable politics, and who, because of the stable background to which they could refer, could write with a sureness which is now no longer possible. For theirs was the Age of Reason, and ours the Age of Unreason; and our 'common sense' is very different from theirs.

III. *The Destructive Element*

But the sense of frustration seen in these topical passages goes deeper, for it is almost the centre of Macneice's work. Macneice is as disillusioned as an Oscar Wilde character, and perhaps the reason is not far to seek, since he is an Irishman. England, Ireland, classical life and literature, Christmas, almost everything is touched, in Macneice's poems, with these belated rays of the Celtic Twilight, in spite of that equally powerful Celtic exuberance which overjoys the reader of such poems as 'Bagpipe Music'. In that finely written 'Eclogue from Iceland' even the inimitable Ghost grouses freely. In the 'Eclogue for Christmas' he gives full rein to his scorn for all the things he dislikes in the modern Americanized Britain; it begins:

> The jaded calendar revolves,
> Its nuts need oil, carbon chokes the valves,

The excess sugar of a diabetic culture
Rotting the nerve of life and literature;
Therefore when we bring out the old tinsel and frills
To announce that Christ is born among the barbarous hills
I turn to you whom a morose routine
Saves from the mad vertigo of being what has been.

Macneice has returned several times to this theme, the paganization of Christ and Christmas, both in 'The Earth Compels' and the 'Autumn Journal', and in almost identical terms. The cheap baubles, the coveted trifles, are symbolic of the uneducated desires, the thwarted longings of the people.

But, on the other hand, Macneice's conception of certain elements of culture is equally negative. In an energetic passage on the Greek world he admits that even there he does not feel at home:

These dead are dead,
And when I should remember the paragons of Hellas
I think instead
Of the crooks, the adventurers, the opportunists,
The careless athletes and the healthy boys. . . .
. . . And the trimmers at Delphi and the dummies at Sparta,
and lastly
I think of the slaves.
And how one can imagine oneself among them
I do not know;
It was all so unimaginably different
And all so long ago.

And elsewhere, true to his Aristotelian rationalism, he makes short work of Plato, or reaches the limits of matter-of-factness when he writes:

Not but what I am glad to have my comforts;
Better authentic Mammon than a bogus God;
If it were not for Lit. Hum. I might be climbing
A ladder with a hod.

This is not so far removed from the attitude of some of

the younger poets who secretly cherished 'culture' but who were so angered at being consistently called 'Left Intellectuals' that they affected to despise their education: Gavin Ewart, for instance, wrote a poem about 'the scurfy, doddering Dons' of Cambridge which reflects such a state of mind.

Macneice lacks one of Auden's stabilizing qualities, his understanding and love of England, but he has written some of his finest poems about remote islands, about Iceland, the Hebrides, in whose mists and grey solitudes he feels most at home. It is evident by this, and his Irish habit of beating his nurse when he writes of his home country:

> Why should I want to go back
>   To you, Ireland, my Ireland?
> The blots on the page are so black
> That they can't be covered with shamrock.

> . . . And she gives her children neither sense nor money
> Who slouch round the world with a gesture and a brogue
>   And a faggot of useless memories.

—it is evident from such things that Macneice is a fundamentally Romantic poet, struggling vainly to repress his feelings, trying to give a casual air to his most sincere opinions, trying, perhaps, to write in a way which is alien to him: in a word, he is damnably Irish.

IV. *Macneice and Eliot*

There is a poem in Macneice's latest book, 'Plant and Phantom', called 'Plurality', which, in spite of its fine conclusion (which contains some of his most feeling lines), shows the drawbacks of the 'common sense' outlook in poetry. This poem is rather like a continuation, in a

serious vein, of certain passages of the 'Autumn Journal'.
Let us compare the following extracts:

(1)   No, perfection means
        Something but must fall unless there intervenes
        Between that meaning and the matter it should fill
        Time's revolving hand that never can be still.
        Which being so and life a ferment, you and I
        Can only live by strife in that the living die,
        And, if we use the word Eternal, stake a claim
        Only to what a bird can find within the frame
        Of momentary flight (the value will persist,
        But as event the night sweeps it away in mist).
                      (Macneice: 'Plurality')

(2)   We had the experience but missed the meaning,
        But approach to the meaning restores the experience
        In a different form, beyond any meaning
        We can assign to happiness. I have said before
        That the past experience revived in the meaning
        Is not the experience of one life only
        But of many generations. (Eliot: 'The Dry Salvages')

(3)   For most of us, there is only the unattended
        Moment, the moment in and out of time,
        The distraction fit, lost in a shaft of sunlight,
        The wild thyme unseen, or the winter lightning
        Or the waterfall, or music heard so deeply
        That it is not heard at all, but you are the music
        While the music lasts.
                    (Eliot: 'The Dry Salvages')

(4)   Those who live in marble or on painted panel know of
    life but a single exquisite instant, eternal indeed in its
    beauty, but limited to one note of passion or one mood
    of calm. (Oscar Wilde: 'The Critic as an Artist')

The subject in these four passages (I include Wilde
here out of curiosity to see what will happen) is very
much the same: the relation of human life to time. The
first four lines of extract (1) should be compared with
the whole of extract (2). In each, three main terms are

used: meaning, experience and time. Macneice's first three lines, although they are a complete statement, I find more difficult to follow than Eliot's first extract, though Eliot's line of thought is really much more complicated. In other words, I find Macneice obscure. Macneice says that 'perfection' has a meaning; and that this informs 'matter'. In other words, he presents Clive Bell's idea of 'Significant Form' to which we are well accustomed. It is less clear, however, in what manner Time can 'intervene' between perfection's 'meaning' and 'the matter it should fill': that is to say, between an abstraction and a concrete. Looking a little farther, all sorts of difficulties arise: does Macneice postulate a perfection independent of matter? does he mean it is not a state but a dynamic power? does he mean that the identification of perfection and matter is only momentary? In as much as so little is clarified in proportion to what is left in doubt, it must be said that Macneice has tried to do more in the space of three lines than he is capable of, or rather, that he has abandoned his subject as soon as it becomes difficult, for the lines immediately following have little relationship to this argument: having postulated that perfection can exist in matter, he states that 'life is a chaos' and proceeds to pursue his own 'meaning'. He might mean simply: 'Perfection cannot last unless it is identified with its object in time', and 'Since Time is ever moving, then Perfection cannot exist for long: it is a momentary state'. I find such lines as these as attractive as the ambiguities of Mallarmé and Empson, but with the difference that those two poets, if one takes pains to follow them, do indicate one definite line which is the reader's reward, whereas Macneice (or perhaps my own stupidity, in which case I shall apologize) leaves me here with a very unpleasant feeling.

Eliot put his case with a Cartesian—though in this

instance it would be more apt to say Bergsonian—clarity:
'Experience is *known* when it occurs, but is not *understood*
until it is past. And when it is past, its meaning is
different from what it really was when it occurred, for
the lapse of time, having changed the individual consciousness, has also changed his conception of the
experience.' That is to say, experience is never understood in its original state; but is enriched by the passage
of time. There is thus an endless chain of experience,
meaning, creating new experience and new meaning, and
owing to man's place both in time and in his relationship
to millions of other beings, his own experience is not only
his own, it is a part of a much vaster experience in space,
time and mind.

It should be evident, by comparing the method used
in the first three lines of (1) and the whole of (2) with
the last part of Macneice's passage (1) and the whole of
(3), that the two poets have used a very similar procedure. First of all the theme is treated in abstract, and
secondly in sensual, terms. Eliot's passage (3) is crammed
with reference to sensual experience, while there is only
one such reference (the bird's flight) in Macneice. On
analysis it is found that Macneice, true to common sense,
proceeds no farther than the conventional 'carpe diem'
philosophy, and in the process recoils from a conception
of 'eternity' which to him might seem irrational. In
other words, he does not bother to pursue the deeper
implications of his theme, contents himself with the
happy image of the 'moment in a bird's flight', then
passes on to another subject. Eliot's method is sounder,
and one which Dryden himself would have applauded.
It is interesting to notice that in his later poems Eliot,
like Dylan Thomas, is striving not to set down a conclusion, but to work towards one. In the process
he does not jib at the labour needed to establish his

c

conception of such terms as time, moment, experience, meaning; he would be quite incapable of a hasty 'if we use the word Eternal', and on the contrary, once faced with such a word, fights until he assigns to it the sense he deems right. So Eliot sets these momentary experiences against a broader background: as he proceeds towards the image on 'being the music', so he proceeds towards a new term, incarnation, and this in turn he had already described as the task of the Saint, whose occupation is

> . . . To apprehend
> The point of intersection of the timeless
> With time.

So he proceeds fearlessly into the unexplored territory from which Macneice suddenly recoiled: these 'moments' of 'incarnation' are but a part realization of the nature of eternity and eternal incarnation:

> Here the impossible union
> Of spheres of existence is actual,
> Here the past and the future
> Are conquered, and reconciled.

There are, then, two main points arising from this rather unpremeditated comparison of Eliot and Macneice. They are, that while Macneice is showing a strong tendency towards didacticism, he has not yet developed what I have called 'sense of direction', 'single-mindedness' and 'sense of balance' in a sufficient degree for him to show the best of his abilities in this direction. He tends to jump from one subject to another, or leaves off a train of thought as soon as it becomes difficult, and there is an inadequate proportion between the cerebral and sensual elements in his argument. I do not suggest he should learn these things from Eliot: it is merely suggested that Eliot has shown that these 'classical' qualities can still be found in twentieth-century writing, even when accompanied by a 'romantic' disposition. The fact here demonstrated is equally applicable to the majority of the younger writers: we have seen, for instance, in Auden's 'New Year Letter' that he has this same tendency to jump from the original path of his thought, especially when it becomes a little thorny or steep.

As for the passage from Oscar Wilde, its analysis I leave to the reader. Wilde's common sense appears unusual because he realized that many problems can be approached from the far end.

V

The above observations are, admittedly, incomplete. So far, the best of Macneice's talent has gone into his shorter poems, some in a metaphysical style, some descriptive poems, one or two classical themes or translations. His group of 'Eclogues' show a definite dramatic sense and a power for verse dialogue which should fit him for the verse drama. It is in the shorter poems that a fine sense of form is most clearly shown, with a clear-cut neatness and little of the facetiousness which spoils his more ambitious efforts. For obvious reasons I refrain from commenting on these shorter poems such as 'Stylite', 'Chess', 'Show', 'Circe', 'Cuckoo'. As the bulk of his work has been topical, common sense and light, I have approached him chiefly from that angle, only to find that his qualities of form and style do not yet show to their best advantage outside the short lyric. His common-sense attitude to life and poetry has led to a series of negations: there is no centre, as yet, to his work. But if he can bring the same qualities to his didactic work as he does to the lyric, or develop his aptitude for drama, he may well prove himself a poet of major importance.

November-December 1941.

GEOFFREY GRIGSON: A MINIATURIST

GEOFFREY GRIGSON is well enough known as journalist, editor of 'New Verse', and as a penetrating art critic, to need no further introduction. It is not surprising that, with his background, he should have tried to bring facts and vision into his poetry, though he was somewhat emphatic in imposing the same attitude on others. He sought a poetry that was concrete, peopled with objects and rooted in materialism. He recoiled with horror from poetry which was personal, and had standards of 'objectiveness' which were occasionally belied by his own poetry and criticism. His bark was much worse than his bite, and alongside of Auden and Co. he fostered Dylan Thomas, George Barker and David Gascoyne.

Grigson's own poems, 'Several Observations' (Cresset Press), have the qualities and defects which such an outlook implies. These thirty-five poems have no great variety. They may be readily divided (for convenience only) into three types of observation: general observations or comments, landscapes and characters. The general observations, chiefly epigrammatic or satiric, are not very satisfying, and are less related to a broad view of life such as might have been expected in a poet of such views and experience. There are a few traces of self-consciousness, but they are disquieting:

> The evil I share, the good I do not do.

The poem 'Per Curiosa ad Astra' is half comment and half character, but rather an intellectualized conversation than a poem. 'Munich, City of Art', a political comment, is a failure as a poem; it conveys little about Munich or about anything, there is little feeling and the satire does not drive home, and it lacks those vital qualities of passion and wit which alone can turn political propaganda into poetry: he writes:

> And in Munich, city of art, Matisse and Delacroix
> And Constable have left the Pinakothek for painters
> The thunder approves.

Political headlines are not enough to people a poem, and reporting and poetry (this poem is not bad reporting) are not synonymous. The same can be said of the poem 'Non-Interveners', save for a fine Spanish sketch in miniature, and the concluding lines. The Spanish parts show his gift as a miniaturist together with a power for controlled but sensual feeling such as is to be found in his best poems:

> and
> In Spain still the brown and gilt of the twisted
> pillar, still the olives, and in the mountains
> the chocolate trunks of cork trees bare from
> the knee, the little smoke from the sides
> of the charcoal-burner's grey tump, the ebony sea-
> hedgehogs in clear water. . . .

Grigson's control of free verse, as shown here, with its slow movement and condensation, is comparable with Spender's. And he can obtain interesting variations of speed and tone, as seen at the end of the same poem:

> And in England the crack-willows, their
> wet leaves reversed by the wind; and
> the swallows sitting different ways like
> notes of music between the black poles on
> the five telephone wires.

It will be noticed that the last line is suddenly breathless, and that the slowness is gained by a clever device in the other lines. Suppress this device and the whole passage moves very differently:

> And in England the crack-willows,
> their wet leaves reversed by the wind;

> and the swallows sitting different ways
> like notes of music between the black poles
> on the five telephone wires.

This device should not be scorned for its simplicity: a writer who will deliberately leave all his minor parts of speech to the end of his lines must have a precise feeling for the telling psychological effect it produces.

Grigson's characters are interesting, and different from those of Auden and Spender and Macneice, who tend to look at people with a dramatic eye. Grigson looks at them rather like a short-story writer, building them into their background. For instance, in that admirable poem 'Forgetful of Europe', the setting of the figures in the midst of some of his most sensual writing is worth observing:

> Think now about all the things which made up
> That place: you noticed first
> Under the plane tree, where the gay
> And white canoes were, the green peppers
> And the black figs on the stall: the countess then
> (Slightly red when we came close
> Between the brown of her body
> And her white bathing dress),
> Her blonde hair pulled off her smart
> Old face, her crimson nails, and not
> A quiver in the guarded bust, as she rose
> With Bull-Dog Drummond from her wicker
> Chair: then from the Countess
> To the chapel, under the pink and white
> Oleanders, up the path between the white walls
> And the soft agrimony; the orchard with
> Scarlet pomegranate flowers, the very deep
> Stream full of light in its curved
> Silk-stocking-coloured limestone bed,
> A sulphur wagtail balanced, where it moved
> Under the mill-house.

It is emotional observation of this type, with its keen

sense of detail and colour, which provides the many highlights in Grigson's work, and it is the most precious contribution he has made to poetry.

Such characters as 'The Office Clerk' are less interesting because their background is less clearly and sympathetically drawn. There is one other character, the Slovene, who in 'Meeting by the Gjulika Meadow' makes one feel that Grigson has a real faculty for observation of people provided he can sympathize with them, and the Slovene, like the Countess, is beautifully related to his background:

> His Zagreb boots were thin, and
> He was taking the plant
>
> Picked by the snow under the
> Nervous frontier to his lovely
>
> Daughter underneath in the farm
> Who was crippled.

This reminds me of those bright and bare descriptions in some of Jules Romains' 'Odes', but it is brilliantly completed with a splash of colour:

> The thunder was sneering, and
> In the lower woods we enjoyed
> The lemon sun again, and the scent
> And magenta of cyclamens.

If there is any doubt about Grigson's sensitiveness to the qualities of words, such lines as these already quoted should serve to dispel it.

Grigson's real talent is limited to this pictorial art. His landscapes, both urban and rural, are unquestionably among the best in our modern poetry, though he lacks those broad, sweeping effects sometimes gained by Edward Thomas, or Auden and Macneice. His landscapes are models of detailed perception. Not that they are lacking in imaginative quality: it is hard to choose among his city views, which are full of sharp outline and colour:

> When the sky has the ominous
> Colours of a bruise, even then
> Bother less over the spirits from the sky
> Than the spirits from the earth.   ('Three Evils')

or:

> . . . consider the clean morning
> The clouds clear off quickly
> Over the roof: the churches
> Turn blue, the windows of the shops
>
> Show their pale smudges
> Because of the sun. . . .

And sometimes the reality of these scenes is absolutely identified (in spite of Grigson's dislike of personal writing) with inner mood, nowhere better, perhaps, than in 'About Now':

> In this bitter season, I discern the reality
> In the bigness of the black leaves
> Against the early light, in the white
> Lilac, between the divided cypress
> In the black-blue air among the pear
> Flowers. . . .

In this and another poem, 'The Hours of the Public Places', Grigson surpasses almost those amazing town-psychology studies of Jules Romains' 'Puissances de Paris'.

The same power of detail is to be found in the rustic landscapes, of which 'The calm sunshine of the heart', one of his most perfect poems, with its complete fusion of feeling and perception, is perhaps the most typical:

> The water falls over the rock,
> The men in armour ride on
> Under the trees: the temple
> Is ruined: the tower is pink.

> The conduit leads to the water-wheel,
> The sun shines on the snow
> On the mountain.   The fishermen
> Pay out the half-circle of their nets,
> The cattle drink in their own
> Reflections. . . .

Grigson is far more convincing as a poet than as a critic.   As a critic he bawls, and tries to club his reader or his enemy into agreement.   As a poet he writes carefully and delicately as one who, knowing his limitations, has determined to turn them into assets.   His poetry is at once sensual, rational, exact and economic, and it is his greatest quality that the first of these is not crushed by the other three.   Grigson has pretended, in his criticism, to set little store by the harmonious qualities of words, but it is evident that he feels their musical value, when he can write 'Magenta of cyclamens', or other lines like 'The wild gladiolus has magenta flowers' or 'And ringed wasp quivering in the rind'.

Grigson might be a restricted poet, but a great deal can be learnt by reading his poems with attention, for he is an excellent craftsman.   There is not another young poet who can surpass him in his almost Stendhalian precision in describing gesture, for instance, as in the following unforgettable picture:

> the men fish
> Swearing in a strange language
> From their curve-end boats
> They heave sprats back on long lines
> To the high nervous watchers.

April 1941.

FREDERIC PROKOSCH: AN EXOTIC

I

FREDERIC PROKOSCH (born 1908) strikes one as a poet who writes with an immaculate but somewhat fatal ease. He has mastered a limited though satisfactory technique, which in its highly conventional style, its florid diction, its elements of mumbo-jumbo, shall I say a sort of inherited and second-hand style, with fluid, uninhibited rhythms, sets him rather aside from his own generation, and thus helps him to hold a sort of balance between the Ancients and Moderns. This ease is not due to any faulty conception of poetry, nor to his precarious affiliation to the 'New Verse' group. He is one of those happy and unhappy people of mixed nationality, a chaos of German, English and Austrian, who has enjoyed what education Germany, France, England and America can afford. This has enabled him to assimilate European culture in a way uncommon to people of his age, though very understandable in a generation which grew up in the shadow of the League of Nations. It can be fairly objected to his poetry that it is too largely cultural and literary, as was the work of Rilke and Mallarmé, which he has obviously read with care but whose concentration he cannot achieve. He has, to balance this praiseworthy fault, a strong lyrical impulse of his own, giving that freshness and enthusiasm which is the peculiar charm of those who write spontaneously. His work is homogeneous, and the same dominant qualities of invention and extravaganza are to be found in his poems as in his novels, 'The Asiatics' and 'The Seven Who Fled'.

FREDERIC PROKOSCH

II. *Lament*

Prokosch's development is another proof of the wisdom of Grigson and the 'New Verse' policy, for he has developed from floweriness to control, from looseness to dignity, without losing any of his better qualities. 'The Assassins' (1936) is not better than, or much different from, what Barker was writing in 1934. Here Prokosch reminisces and resumes pitilessly, serving a laborious apprenticeship to the more lasting poets of the late nineteenth century; his adjectives lusciously accumulated though sometimes primly ordered, his phrases pompously inverted; but with all this there can be little doubt that the book was one of the best first collections which appeared in the 'thirties. On a larger scale there is one serious fault: that some of his poems drift aimlessly, with no clear impulse or direction, the poem achieving no definite centre and therefore having no form to speak of. This is to be seen in such poems as 'The Voyage' (the too familiar and by now depressing Auden and Spender theme), a poem of five five-line stanzas which forms one very interesting but rambling sentence. The enormous sentence has its legitimate place in the enormous poem— in 'Paradise Lost', for instance, where it is masterfully used—but it is one of the blights of lyric poetry, a trap for the young who can control neither their emotion nor their stanza, and a wicked temptation for the old who have nothing or too much on their minds. Such a poem reminds one of the worst vice of Hugo, Verlaine, Shelley and Wordsworth, in works which are like immense glossy apples, delicious to look at but depressingly watery when bitten. And we find in this same poem one of Prokosch's characteristic devices, which he has repeated so often that I cannot read a poem where this is done without thinking of Prokosch. This is a deliberate

and always effective shortening of the last line of each
stanza, which gives a pathetic, constricting effect:

> And finally, having come to the world's long boundary,
> We waited, but saw nothing, waited, but no
> Sound broke the huge stillness; and slowly turning
> Saw only stars like snow on the endless prairie
>   And a sea of snow.

Coupled with the numerous negations, heavy internal
assonances and the peculiar repetition of the 'snow'
image, the pathos here becomes bathetic and recalls the
worst of Spender. Prokosch uses this trick in seven or
eight of the poems in this book, some five or six in his
second book, and seven in his third. Not that it really
matters, only he seems to have decided to class himself
beyond doubt as a primarily elegiac poet. This is one's
first impression, though it might be mistaken. It is certain,
however, that his poems which succeed usually have that
atmosphere of nostalgia, desolation, frustration and lament
which we associate with such names as Dowson. In this first
volume the lamentation is rather thin and undirected:

> I found them lying on the shore,
> Sweet shapes, pearl-lipped and crescent-eyed:
> Night after night their hands implore
> Pathetic mercies at my side. . . .

('The Dolls'. Any of the Sitwells might have written
this.)

> Lowering her lids through night she sees
> Towers, pavilions, balconies,
> Cities whose tender millions move
> Through the vast labyrinths of love,
> Each in its own peculiar pain,
> Lost on the hot inhabited plain.

('Andromeda.' This poem is charmingly weak. A
cheap trick shows up some of its faults:

> Cities whose vast millions move
> Through tender labyrinths of love,

> Each on the inhabited plain
> Lost in its hot peculiar pain.)

But all his poems have one outstanding quality which defies the cheap trick used above. Prokosch, unlike many of the younger poets, has what is to my mind one of the first requisites of a poet, the gift of a sensitive ear and a feeling for the purely sensual harmonies of words. Dr Richards's experiment, by which he tried to discredit the sensual harmony of words by putting together soundful combinations of nonsense-syllables, proved nothing at all, except the difference between sound with meaning and sound without meaning, of which nobody needs any illustration. Let us take a few lines of Carroll to illustrate this point:

> 'Twas brillig, and the slithy toves
> Did gyre and gimble in the wabe;
> All mimsy were the borogoves
> And the mome raths outgrabe.

Thirteen words out of these twenty-three are normal, and normally used. Of the rest, almost all of them are not far removed from a word which in this context would make sense: 'brillig', brilliant; 'slithy', slimy; and so on. These lines are poetry—and here Dr Richards is in agreement—only in so far as the sounds used approximate to a meaning. But it will be noticed that we apprehend the meaning of these lines only because the sound of the words approximates to the sound as well as the 'meaning' (which is indivisible from sound) of the words. Our first reaction to words, since they are presented to us through a sensual medium, is largely sensual. That is to say, that in poetry the sensual, or what some choose to call the 'musical', element is of considerable importance, and a poet without ear will not give urgency to his meaning by that sensual appeal which is one of the essential qualities of poetry. In opposing the school who laid stress on sound to the neglect of meaning, Dr Richards was quite right, but went to the opposite extreme in denying sound its value in poetry.

I do not propose to analyse the harmonics of Prokosch's poetry: what I mean is that it is not a purely destructive criticism to say that he weeps musically over everything, as well over the (very Audenesque) 'Empty Provinces', or the cliffs of Norway, or the world as a whole:

> I gaze from the edge of vast America
> Towards the three continents twined in a common terror
> Whose creatures still implore their nocturnal heroes:
> A phrase towards the infinite, there as here: no more.
>
> ('The Piazza')

He also weeps tunefully beside 'The Adriatic', replays the Byronic Hero or Wandering Jew in 'The Azores':

> For here too we shall wander, here too the anxious and old
> Will pass on their way, here too, fingers peaked in a
> Forgotten gesture of prayer, lips imploring, bewildered
>   As dolls, and cold,
>   We too shall wander. . . .

And so he continues, weeping at Port Said, in China, in Utah, and between times into the Caspian and the Atlantic. Enough of this: what does it mean? It means, first of all, that Prokosch is as good at what I call 'Psychic Geography' as Auden, or even better because his range is wider. It is said that he wrote a travel-book about the Near East without going there: I am quite willing to believe it, and that the book would be good. I know of no poet, unless we rummage among the great, such as Shakespeare and Milton, in whose poems the child-amazing wonders of the world are so constantly and convincingly present as in Prokosch. This is a fair sign of a poetic disposition, this type of sympathetic and creative imagination which enabled Rimbaud to write his 'Drunken Boat' long before he had seen the sea.

With such a psychic eye and delicate ear he has all the possibility of being a sort of English Rimbaud, though I should prefer to believe that in Prokosch the English have discovered their own Verlaine (who, it must be remembered, did one or two things which were beyond Rimbaud).

The second meaning of Prokosch's lamentation is, that he has given a purely intuitive interpretation of the mal-de-siècle which weighed so heavily on our poets between the two wars. Perhaps he has been a little wiser than most in refraining from analysing, explaining and apologizing for his nostalgia and tears. His poems are the essence of this feeling, intensified by the psychic geography and by another quality, that sense of mystery which always distinguishes the Romantic poet. Take his flamboyant (and no doubt best-selling) titles to start with: 'The Assassins', 'The Carnival', 'The Asiatics', 'The Seven Who Fled', 'Death at Sea'. These send a thrill down the spine, a thrill sustained by the no less evocative titles of his poems: 'The Masks', 'The Tragedians', 'The Gothic Dusk', 'The Conspirators'. . . . Prokosch has, before the poem has been read, already managed to excite and hush his reader. And this evocative flair glows throughout his poems:

> Black and still under the Siberian heaven
> Lies the lake: rise the reeds: sleep the herons.
>
> ('The Watcher')

> All over Africa they lay awake,
> The panther-eyed tribes, and fearing the increasing twilight
> Hours, suspecting magical

> Modes to destroy, saw in each foreign whisper
> Signs of a vast invasion, shadows terribly
> Trampling the perilous dusk.   ('Daybreak')

This gift for suggestive description often leans to the macabre, but Prokosch has instinctively refused to develop fully his gift for the macabre. In his subsequent development he made more sparing but very effective use of the musical, psychic, and what for lack of a better term I must call mysterious methods of suggestion which gave value to his first work.

III. *Directions*

His second book, 'The Carnival' (1938), was on the whole much happier, showing a greater sense of the positive values of life, and a much greater capacity for enjoyment. The book contains one of the best emotional statements of the social crisis of the 'thirties, his eight-page 'Ode', which first appeared in 'New Verse'.

There is also a greater power of concentration in these poems than was to be found in 'The Assassins'. Some of the pieces are slight, but these, perhaps, are those which will never lose their first attraction, poems like 'Evening', the 'Songs', 'Bathers' and 'Nocturne'. His own experience emerges best through these shorter poems, which are moments of intense realization which help us to class him almost as a neo-symbolist. Take, for instance, 'Evening':

> Pears from the boughs hung golden,
> The street lay still and cool,
> Children with books and satchels
> Came sauntering home from school;
> The dusk fled softly inward
> Across each darkening sill,
> The whole sweet autumn slumbered,
> The street lay cool and still:
>
> The children moved through twilight,
> The village steeple gleamed,
> Pears from their boughs hung trembling,
> And suddenly it seemed,

Shaken with such a wildness
Of terror and desire,
My heart burst into music
And my body into fire.

This type of poem should theoretically be easy to write:
it is what poets like W. H. Davies spent a whole lifetime
trying to write and succeeded only once in twenty years.
All the baggage of an outmoded poetic diction is here:
'golden pears', 'dusk', 'sweet', 'slumbered', 'twilight',
'wildness', 'desire', 'music', 'fire'. This looks like a
dictionary of clichés, and they are of course words which
at once lend themselves to any novice who starts writing
poetry. But in this poem they are obviously pardonable
and necessary: the whole experience, one of innocence
and sensual delight, could only be expressed in this most
traditional language because it must be realized that in
this poem the poet, so seized by this scene of peace and
childhood, speaks *as* a child, identifies the scene with his
own childhood, and as a result uses the language which,
as a boy, he was accustomed to associate with all poetic
expression. Had this not been done, I think the experience
could not have been so complete and true as it obviously
is in this poem. This very simple experience is paranoiac,
having that sense of identification, that transcended
atmosphere, created (strange conjunction!) by Dali in
his painting and Yeats in some of his poems. It will also
be noticed that in this poem Prokosch's familiar nostalgia
has now been turned to a creative purpose, in a positive
direction, that of participation, and it is this participation,
this new social consciousness, which makes 'The Carnival' so less literary than 'The Assassins'.

'The Carnival' is the book of an individualist, wrestling
as though for the first time with the realities of his social
environment. The mystery of 'The Assassins', exotic
and obscure, had all the latent horror and fear of the

unknown, but this second book portrays the fear and knowledge of the known. The exoticism and love of ruins, the lament for lost childhood, is completed first of all by a very logical yearning for something more real, more solid, as seen in the lines:

> O, dreams mean desolation, dreams mean grief,
> I know: and still with energy and love
> I dream that like Magellan I might move
> Through straits and wishes to some vast belief.
>
> ('New Year's Eve')

It is not surprising, after this avowal, that most of these poems are in a sense the expression of a negation. Many of the poems ask questions, but furnish no answers: the type of poems which one usually finds depressing. In many others there is the logical criticism of the negative elements of human existence: 'Sun-Girdled Heliogabalus'—

> And through the imperial vessels
> The great corruption spread

—or 'The Conquerors', a denunciation of Machiavelli, Zaharoff and all the powers of oppression:

> Gorilla, plague and tempest
> Darken all Europe's sky:
> Many have sought the oracle
> But there was no reply.
> Through history's savage wood
> Still roam the burning eyes,
> The mind which swells on blood,
> The love which kills with lies.

It is obvious that much of this writing springs from purely cultural experience rather than feeling, and the presence of Oscar Wilde is felt in the last line ('For each man kills the thing he loves', etc.). And the truth is that in the real sense of the term Prokosch, like Eliot and Pound and so many who have tried to understand

Europe culturally, through the past, instead of the present, has missed something, and has failed to write any poetry (save the shorter lyrics already mentioned) bearing directly on social matters, which might appeal to any but a very select audience drawn exclusively from the intelligentsia. He belongs, like Rilke and Mallarmé, to a very rarefied and privileged, over-refined caste of poets. Yearning for a 'vast belief', the belief he found was, to my mind, not vast enough. It is a belief in the cream of civilization, unaccompanied by a love of flesh and blood, sweat and toil which go to the making of such culture. This is evident in his magnificent 'Ode', which is unpolitical and unsocial in the broadest sense, but otherwise a brilliant defence of cultural and humanitarian values. This 'Ode' is in many ways like Auden's 'Spain', but whereas Auden, in this as in all his poems, always lays emphasis on human activities, and expresses them through motor and social imagery, Prokosch has greater sensual perception, but is much more general, florid and literary. At the same time, his poem is so much more limited that it is more of a personal statement than Auden's, its limitations being those of his own rather intellectual outlook. The cultural survey with which the poem begins is excellently done, but not particularly in his own style:

> Centaurs once roamed these woods and Vandals slumbered
> Above these streams. And then came the chaste basilicas
>   Where scrolls and piety hissed like the autumn
> Leaves. And then the dactyls of engines.

The Centaurs are his own; the idea of Vandals 'slumbering' shows a certain looseness of definition; 'hissed' does not seem particularly apt, save for the leaves; while the 'dactyls of engines' is pure Day Lewis. But once this is said it still remains that, though there is none of that clear definition in which Auden excels, there is a general pleasantness in this writing which is very refreshing. It is because Prokosch has a tender and sentimental attitude to the past (rather like Flecker) that he can write about it in this agreeable meandering way: things happen sweetly and gently for Prokosch which happen brutally and startlingly in Auden. Personally I like this way of dealing with the past, though I feel it is to a degree false; like Banville, whom Baudelaire described as 'The poet of hours of happiness', Prokosch picks out, deliberately, all the plums of his childhood and of his historical sense, omitting the suffering, the slavery and exploitation which lay behind those things:

> Once as a child I gazed at the evening streets
> Where boys like birds of another age went weaving
> Their sunlit paths.   The fountains were magic, and all
> 　The spires and maxims of towering Europe.
>
> Then, the discovery of the body; of Athens
> And the gymnasium.   The javelin and the discus
> Shone in my palms and plans for a clear and living
> 　America.   These were the symbols of power.

The justification, on an aesthetic plane, is that all the poem is quotable: this 'Ode' is perhaps the most intoxicating and sensuous poem produced in the 'thirties. It is the swan-song of Europe, and for that reason, while it is certainly less urgent, less an incentive to action, than Auden's 'Spain', less true to the horrible tragedy of modern Europe than Auden's poem, less realistic altogether, the fact that it is a sensual realization of loss, and that the primitive values of poetry are so maintained, makes it *purer* poetry. I like to recall the macabre element of the fourth part of this poem, or the stylization of the fifth:

> O happy the huntsman returns to his native wood,
> The warrior home from the Indies, the whittling sailor
> In front of his cottage, listening to the expected
> Voice of the evening bells encircling the valley:

Happy the watchman wandering down his lanes, and
The fisherman spreading his nets on the scalloped beaches:
Happy the lark and the whale: and the motionless angler
Marking the trout and the nodding life of the sense.

It is a long time since we have had a poet who could
write so easily, so richly and simply at once. If the poem
is written, in a sense, from too great a height, so that the
Spanish war which prompted it is quite dwarfed or
obscured, this poem is another reminder, to those who
ask now for 'war poetry', that the poets of the 'thirties
realized very well what was happening long before this
war actually 'started'.

IV

The book 'Death at Sea' develops satisfactorily in the
direction of this broad human feeling which is characteristic of Prokosch's approach to maturity. There is, in
these new poems, no sign of any new element, any new
interest, any new experiment developing in his mind or
technique. It is doubtful whether Prokosch could ever
write a long poem, that is to say one longer than his
eight-page 'Ode'. He has no need to, for his intuitive
grasp of momentary feeling and experience is a quality
which debars him at once from any more ambitious or
didactic type of writing in verse. At the same time, he
seems to have reacted with great sanity to the war, and
has not made a fool of himself as many poets who rely
less on their feelings have done. His judgment of the
matter is, I think, very true to that of his own generation:

Miraculous presences
Whose breath disturbs the silence of ponds at evening,
Now summon forth like a ringing of bells the wildness
In all our hearts: the little hands fade away,
And catching our breath as the vision gathers meaning
And the deafening music quickens, we know that somewhere
We shall start again. Though not easily. And not soon.

With so much that is good, these 'miraculous presences', of which we should like to know a little more, this mysterious 'vision', the symbolic 'music', are the old evasions which have beset Prokosch since he started printing his poetry. But such of his war poems as 'Soliloquy' and 'The Country Houses' are among the best so-called war poems produced in this conflict. If vices of language persist, his later poems are achieving that firmness of outline which his earlier work lacked. This spoilt child of an over-civilized, or should we say a culture-ridden, Europe has those faults and merits of poetic style which make him something of a modern Keats.

July 1941.

KENNETH ALLOTT: AN INTELLECTUAL

I. *Formation*

KENNETH ALLOTT is one of the most intelligent of the younger poets; he has undoubtedly a finer literary background, a sharper wit and a keener sense of morality than most. He shares with others a tendency towards preciousness and a liking for telescoped imagery. As a student his poems were too closely modelled on Eliot, with a little Aquinas, Molnar, Donne and Laforgue thrown in. They betrayed already a strong liking for monologue and elegant dialogue, as well as a graveyard imagery, and it was only logical that he should write two very sound theses on seventeenth-century poets, two or three ingenious plays and a lively conversational novel, before writing 'London Letters' and teaching. He has since written a good book on Jules Verne. Geoffrey Grigson began printing him in 'New Verse' in 1935. Since the 'New Verse' outlook was not watertight, he was able to dally finally with Surrealism in 1936, when some of his work appeared in 'Contemporary Poetry and Prose'. In the meantime he had evolved from Catholicism to a certain agnosticism and an awakening interest in the society about him. He is another of his generation to eschew the religious and political props of Eliot and Auden.

When his first volume of poems appeared in 1938 (Hogarth Press) it was noticeable, by comparing the texts of his poems as they had appeared in reviews with their form in the book, that many of them had been changed for the better, especially in an emendation of preciousness and in a toning down of the Surrealism. It was also apparent that Allott had retained no poems written earlier than 1935; that at least two poems appearing in 'New Verse' in 1935 were not reprinted; and that, with only one or two 1935 poems, about six 1936 poems, the bulk of the book represented only two years' work, 1937 and 1938. But in spite of the limits he set to his selection, the literary background of his work is still evident in the poems presented. Eliot's finger is in 'Quicksilver':

> And the future hidden
> And the future hidden
> And the future hidden from us.

But those lines were not half so Eliot in the original version ('New Verse', April 1936), and indeed only nine lines of the original poem have been retained. And Donne also peeps out of one or two poems, especially

> Hold up your head, and at the eleventh hour
> Let the fancy feelings, the spiral failings go.

> Slugged by ungainly distance you and I
> Beneath the same stars separately lie,
> But let our worlds grow singular, and let
> Those parts be mapped some do, we would, forget.

('End of a Year')

Donne scarcely wrote that better, though he would hardly have said 'fancy feelings' and 'ungainly distance'.

To abandon the source-hunt, some readers might detect a little Auden here and there: the schoolmaster Auden in 'Quicksilver' (the only frankly derivative poem), the sight-seeing Auden in 'Parable' (an early poem, 'New Verse', 1935), the Spanish Auden in 'Men Walk Upright', Laura Riding in the 'Gnomic Verses', and Surrealism in 'Azrael'.

II. *Characteristics*

The dramatist and moralist in Allott are strong, and account for weaknesses which have a certain appeal. It is that, like the Ancient Mariner, he holds his reader by the hand and makes him listen. The majority of the poems are 'addressed', very few of them being self-intentioned personal lyrics. There is always an audience in these poems, usually a drawing-room audience and sometimes less intelligent than the poet himself. Thus:

> *I show you* this city as a Victorian whatnot
> Set among weak and stingy scenery.

> *Give me* my sooty town's spasmodic breathing.

> *I tell you straight* that seeing is believing.

> *Out my friends*
> And mix in the heat with the smell of the other slaves.
> ('The Museum')

> How will you enter? There are no entrances.
> How will you leave it? *I tell you* there is no exit.
> ('Privacy')

> So far, *my friend*, a twirling of moustaches.
> ('The Infinite Regress')

Another characteristic of Kenneth Allott's verse is the preciosity to which many of his reviewers objected. This is likely to decline. It occurs largely in odd choices of adjectives and fin-de-siècle verbs. As for the verbs, there is only one which really irritates:

> And the sea goes mincing back into the sunset.
> ('The Statue')

> The cats mince out of hiding and begin to live.
> ('Love in the Suburbs')

'Cats mince' is scarcely happy. The adjectival preciousness has a certain charm to which we are all victims:

'mild laboratories', 'smoky wishes', 'perfunctory west', 'waxen certainties' (in the original version it was 'waven certainties'), 'evangelical donkeys', 'ridiculous years', 'notable flowers', 'snobbish dark'. Occasionally these tricks ('uxorious streams') have a seventeenth- or eighteenth-century flavour: at no time are they the type of verbal invention one expects to find in 'New Verse'.

Finally, Allott is more than usually fond of the 'list' or 'catalogue' device in writing his poems. This consists of piling up objects and images and activities in a stupendous way until the poet's fatigue obliges him to stop. Sometimes it consists of taking a refrain, which is repeated at regular intervals and each time evokes a new set of images. There is nothing wrong with the catalogue poem; some of the best parts of Virgil and Shakespeare are of this type. The twentieth century has perfected the catalogue poem for all time. What else are Pound's 'Cantos', Lewis's 'One-Way Song', Macneice's 'Autumn Journal' and even Auden's 'Spain', but catalogue poems? It will be noticed from this list that the catalogue poem can take many forms, and not one of those mentioned is not packed with interest. Pound's catalogue is justified by a vast historical background (history is cataloguing); Lewis's is a series of likes and dislikes (criticism of a kind is cataloguing); Macneice's is a personal bulletin (diaries are catalogues); Auden's is a culture-survey with a historical and geographical background (surveying is cataloguing) . . . The list could be lengthened with Grigson's 'Several Observations' (reporting is cataloguing) and D. H. Lawrence's 'Birds, Beasts and Flowers' (the very title is a catalogue), and so on. It appears, then, that the term catalogue is nothing to be ashamed of, for it is inevitable as soon as the poët steps out of the hoop of the compact lyric and looks about him. It is avoidable only by those who deliberately restrict their horizon (Imagists and Symbolists), or those who sublimate their personal impressions, sightseeing and literary gleanings, in the drama and the novel.

The justification of catalogue poems is how they are done. Allott's differ from the above by being nearer the Surrealist's amazing lists of disparate objects. In such poems as 'Any Point in the Circumference', 'Offering', 'Historical Grimace', 'Azrael', 'Calenture' and 'Against the Clock' he has catalogued in various ways. In that splendid lyric, 'Offering', the rhythmic flow and integrating feeling of which place it among his best poems, the poet offers the world as his love-gift. The extraordinary things seem doubly odd out of their context, but in the poem itself a great depth of sympathy and feeling weaves together a thousand painful realities and intangible dreams. The movement towards the end is very fine:

> I would offer you so much more if you would turn
> Before the new whisper in a forgiving hour.
> Let all the wild ones who have offended burn,
> Let love dissemble in a golden shower;
> Let not the wind whistle, nor the sea rave,
> But the treasure be lapped forever in an unbroken wave.
>
> There is nothing that I would not offer you,
> My silken dacoit, my untranslatable,
> Whether in the smug mountains counting the stars
> Or crossing the gipsy's palm in the Eastern fairs,
> With so much that it is difficult to say
> Before the frigid unpeculating hours
> Shall drive the foreign devil to the sea.

The poem 'Azrael' is more Surrealist (belonging to the 1936 excursion), and is an attempt to convey the idea of death through a hundred images. It is less successful and a little forced in places, but again contains some

excellent realist touches which show the poet remains
at all times close to life:

> Their angular shadows pitching into the storm
> Above the bleak and weary cottages
> Where the soft candle dies in the hostile gloom,
> And the children bury their heads in the clothes, in the
>   darkness.

Although the development is logical enough, the
Surrealist shock is produced from time to time by
unexpected contrasts:

> Death is an ancient cross by an inland shore,
> Death the sophisticated district-visitor,
> Death as a rusty broken-ribbed umbrella,
> Death as a bright and poisonous miasma.

This sort of poem has no logical end. One or two
other list poems do not seem successful because the theme
does not emerge. 'Any Point in the Circumference' is
a patchwork of beautiful things, but it appears to me
more like two poems joined together than a single unity.
This was not so obvious in the first version ('New Verse',
February-March 1937), but is more so in the volume,
where a new stanza was interpolated in the middle of
the poem:

> O little child of love,
> The moon grows to the full,
> The dark is fearful but the moon will light you;
> You shall go over the hills before you die
> With a loved one beside you.

This should serve as a good instance of Allott's frequent
combination of morbidity and tenderness, but it cannot
be said to have clarified the poem. The same applies to
'Historical Grimace', where the fourth stanza is hardly
integrated into the poem. It may be deliberate. It may
be (in this poem) Allott's way of indicating the external

and internal planes of the individual's life in conflict
with each other.

III. *Attitudes*

One must look in vain for a positive outlook in such
a poet. What there is to be found is a reflection of the
intellectual anarchism of a generation, an individualist
to the core, disgusted and disillusioned with what he sees
about him, with no desire to live in the past, nor even
in the present, no hope in the future, no political or
religious creed to act as a stabilizing or reassuring
influence. So he is above all ironic, and his tentative
carpe-diem is a straw-clutching reaction from an unknown
tomorrow.

'Aunt Sally Speaks' is one of his best poems, very
moving to read and with an impressive rhythmical movement. In it he indicates in negative terms the mentality
of an epoch,

> Who have been educated out of naïve responses,
> The hoodoo of love, the cinderella of class. . . .

> Wiseacres playing with terrible dolls in the twilight.

> What shall we do who cannot place a candle
> Before the ikon of the future, nor yet acquiesce
>   Unconsciously in habit;

> To whom the actor's gesture, the preacher's word
> Are not enough, being at all times too conscious
> Of the shortcomings of motive, who refuse drugs
>   And the tail-spin of madness . . .

The poem is admirably constructed and the accumulation
of evidence and analysis maturely done. The individualist has no solution, and the poem lacks that
roundness which it might have achieved in the hands of
anyone with a faith (impossible, of course, as no poet with

a faith could have written it), and it ends with a gasp of frustration, a squib of preciosity:

> What shall we do with our hardened arteries
> Under the zeppelin shade of catastrophe
> But emulate the gloss and selfishness of china
>   Till the clocks fly away.

The poem appeals aesthetically but is unsatisfying as a statement of an attitude. It first appeared in 1937 and it is evident that the poet himself was not satisfied, for he took up the same subject again, and in the identical rhythmic pattern, so that the longer 'Men Walk Upright' might be read as a continuation of it. 'Men Walk Upright' ('Twentieth Century Verse', July 1938), his most solid poem, seems to have been written after seeing Auden's 'Spain' and Prokosch's eight-page 'Ode' ('New Verse', March 1938). The historical-geographical survey is Audenesque, but the tone of the cross-questioning is more like Prokosch, who tackled almost the same aspects of the problem as Allott. It would be presumption to compare the poems, and perhaps it is cheek to suggest that they have anything in common save their date. But Allott's and Prokosch's poems were two of the best of their type in 1938, a year when poets were writing long and serious poems about European civilization and thoughtfully examining their own consciences. Their broad view reflected a prevalent and permanent state of mind, and now that the war they foresaw is here, they can still be read with profit.

'Men Walk Upright' is Allott's most serious attempt at facing up to reality. It is a poem of almost complete disillusion, even in its broadest, least political and least local aspects:

> The necessary light awakening the seasons and cities
> Shapes the anarchic continents from the dark,

> But gives no comfort: rather, like an ex-friend,
>   Cuts you more deeply.

After a jibe at 'freedom', which, according to the poet, gives merely

> the right to accumulate
> Dust on library shelves, to be proud of an accent,
>   To decide in no question,

only the scientist and the artist, for their integrity and detachment, receive any praise, but even they appear not indifferent to the good things of this life and are represented as fundamentally egotists. The rest of the poem reveals a social awareness which has since increased in Allott's verse, a strong appreciation of poverty and misery which is very moving. But Allott is not like those who, realizing their sense of humanitarianism and fair play, imagine they are world-savers. Having disclosed Europe and civilization bad to the core, the poet as individualist has nothing more to offer than that same paralysis of will which led to the present war:

> Is this the end? The distant stars are ironic
> To see so much self-torture. I am like you.
> The blackbirds sing and I see no end of agony,
>   The pink and white blossom

> Spangles the chestnuts, the theatres pour into the streets
> The unimaginative. And the earth renews
> In Europe its solar gaiety, and the earth moves on
>   To no destination.

'To no destination.' It seems fit enough that uprooted writers like Eliot and Prokosch should lament nostalgically over a disintegrating Europe they never possessed or understood. But the European, it seems, has scarcely the right to be so detached, and for this reason this poem excited the bile of one or two reviewers. It is not difficult to reply to them, for it is the poem of a man who has lost religion and who has stepped suddenly into a world of fact and found no adjustment. The cheerful politics of the unreflective does not come easily. Allott is to be thanked for having so potently crystallized the outlook of thousands who have been overwhelmed by forces not of their own making and beyond their control.

There are one or two other 'political' poems in the collection, which also indicate that by 1938 Allott had found no positive outlook. Such are 'The Museum', a jibe at Oxford; 'The Plutocrats', a jibe at the rich, though it seems that they are not psychologically understood (for instance, a Marxist would see them as being, as much as the poor, victims rather than villains of a system); and 'Exodus', a jibe at the incompetent leaders of Europe. Other poems on similar themes show no more indication of a positive attitude. The time theme is present in 'Quicksilver' ('Enjoy the present for it won't last long'), 'To Die Clean', 'End of a Year' ('The generations summer in our stead'), 'Exodus' ('The nebulae climbing nowhere in the dark'), and 'Memento Mori' ('the leaves / Cannot, any more than we can, tell which way they are going'). Only the love poems, and especially 'Offering' and 'Calenture', show any zest in life. Finally, the humorous poems, which are steadily gaining Allott a wider reputation, show the same ironic attitudes to society and time. The 'Lament for a Cricket XI' not only shows all time's cruel tricks, it is also a lament for a class of society, the lower-middles: 'The Professor' and 'Love in the Suburbs' show the smallness and futility of life in a way which is satiric, not funny. Indeed, all the humorous poems (see also 'Love and Herbert Spencer', 'Municipal Myth' and 'Heroes and Hero-Worship') are caricatural and lack that balm which is the saving element of humour. They are not so 'light' as they look. Allott has still deeply ingrained in him the pessimism of an earlier generation, the sorrow of exiles and the square poles in round holes of T. S. Eliot. For the reason that he is nearer humour than Eliot, and does not want to 'integrate' himself into Europe whether by respecting the King or going to church, he is nearer to Laforgue than Eliot was. And, of course, being an Englishman, he is even more of an individualist than Laforgue. Individualism is a wide term, however, and in this case it means not self-contained, but self-dissatisfied, self-examining. Modern poetry as a whole is introspective, but Allott differs from many of his generation in his unbending severity, even in humour, his refusal (in spite of his injunction 'Try not to edge beyond your earned three weeks') to enjoy thoroughly the present, and his refusal (in spite of his horror at Oxford smugness, plutocrats and slums) to accept any political remedy. It is in this sense especially, in his self-appointed capacity of 'outsider', that Allott is at once an 'observer' poet and a moralist. The fate of the observer, like that of Tiresias, is to see and suffer all but to conclude nothing, unless it be to acquire wisdom. As Dylan Thomas expressed it so well,

> Bound by a sovereign strip we lie,
> Watch yellow, wish for wind to blow away
> The strata of the shore and drown red rock;
> But wishes breed not, neither
> Can we fend off the rock arrival. . . .

IV. *Observation*

In a number of 'New Verse' in 1938 Kenneth Allott made some remarks about poetry and society which are only partly in accord with his practice as a poet. When he said, 'I suggest diffidently that morals are important in poetry', he was certainly speaking for himself. He

D

wrote also: 'I do not know what I mean by society; perhaps Communism, Liberalism, Transcendentalism, Capitalism, Fascism, Humanitarianism.' This is very much in accord with the conclusions to which his poems drive us: that he is a social agnostic. But his poetry does not reveal any conception of society as a collection of 'isms', nor any clear picture of any 'ism': the general impression is blurred and quite free of watertight compartments. And even when, after rejecting the broad view of society, Allott offers instead the observation of the world in miniature, in the idea of 'Doing something for your street', he is expressing, as poets too often do, not a fact about his poems, but a wish. The very attractive idea of doing something for one's street is quite irrelevant when tried by an examination of his poems. He is interested in much more than his street, and his poems owe their interest rather to a wide moral and cultural background which classes his work as primarily that of a world-conscious intellectual.

The poems in Allott's 1938 volume are not exclusively that of an observer, and I doubt whether they would be so good if they were. They are founded upon realities, and that is the justification of his attachment to 'New Verse'. But those realities are broad, and not merely local flora and fauna. Life is certainly full of objects and events, but man peoples it convincingly with fairy-tales, dreams, reflections and a thousand abstractions. Allott uses objects and events subsidiarily, as convenient references for his feelings and ideas. What he observes best is his feelings ('Men Walk Upright', 'Aunt Sally Speaks') and his memories ('Declaration of Independence'—printed in 'Programme', 1936), the sensation of falling asleep ('Lullaby', 'Calenture', 'The Statue'), the sensation of falling in love ('Offering'), the mental attitudes of people ('Lovers we Need', 'Heroes and Hero-

Worship'). To take a few instances, 'Sunday Excursion,' which looks at first like an attempt at reporting, is something much deeper: Nelson's column sets him thinking on heroes and slogans, and it is the moralist who tells us anything in this poem:

> Ponder how close to the houses the darkness begins.
> Disaster and laughter are both Greek gifts to the air.
>   Will you breed drays?
> But who shall die like an opera this or next year?
>   And why do your heroes
>   Sulk or like celluloid flare?

And in 'Exodus', a topical poem on the state of Europe during the Spanish war, and which begins in such a fine movement of indignation, there occurs this piece of 'realism' which, on analysis, is transparently literary:

> And I imagine sometimes at night emerging
> The stunted pasty wonder of the slum
> Like a cracked bicycle frame
> On which a short vocabulary is hung. . . .

The image, brilliantly sketched, is not developed and is in fact suppressed by the last line, which belongs to an entirely different category of observation. The first idea, of dilapidation, is swallowed up by the second, the idea of class, which at once throws the reader into abstract considerations of culture, education and inarticulateness, which belong rather to the moralist and short-circuit both the feelings of pity and disgust which were first invoked.

There is no doubt whatever that Allott has a keen eye, as keen as any that is to be found in 'New Verse'. But there are many ways of seeing: in 'Memento Mori', for instance, nothing is seen separately or distinctly, but bulked together and confused as in recollection. In the middle of this panorama the moralist and intellectual again appear:

> Time trickled sluggishly past the Piltdown man
> To offer us only today a meal of doom.
> Behind the rain a blind girl is practising scales
> Like an unfortunate beauty.   It is not beautiful.
> At Geneva the lake looks coldly at the people. . . .

It should be obvious from such a poem that the intellectually complete man in Allott, who has read Laforgue, heard of the Piltdown man and the League of Nations, cannot be tied down to 'doing something for his street' in the form of mass-observation of a suburban avenue.

1940.

DYLAN THOMAS: A PIONEER

I. *Points of Contact*

Dʏʟᴀɴ Tʜᴏᴍᴀs is one of the most promising of the poets under thirty, but he has suffered through catching the public eye a little too early, which resulted in unfounded criticism by both his supporters and detractors. He was promising in 1934 ('Eighteen Poems: Parton Press) and promising in 1936 ('Twenty-five Poems': Dent). To those who have followed his production since then he is still promising, and this premature estimate of him is being made to clarify the nature of that promise.

For many people his poems are puzzles, seeming to offer at first reading no more than a forbidding cliff, impenetrable to reason, from which there jut great crags of capricious imagery. Some people (notably Miss Sitwell) read him for his sound, but though the words peal fully and roundly, the rhythms are monotonous enough to make this pall. But many a good poet is monotonous. The only satisfactory approach seems to be to plumb these images and verbal din and see what lies beyond.

The poems, especially in the 1934 and 1935 volumes, seem to have three noticeable points of contact. Discussion of the Metaphysicals, Sitwellism and Surrealism are irrelevant. The dominant points of contact seem to be James Joyce, the Bible and Freud. The personal habits of language and mythology of Dylan Thomas can readily be identified through these three sources. The first is linguistic, the second mythological, the third psycho-pathological, the key to his interpretation of his world.

II. *Language*

It is agreed that James Joyce's language in 'Ulysses' is simple enough. It appears difficult only when sentences and parts of sentences do not appear logically related. 'Ulysses' is the masterpiece of the unexpected: the element of surprise, so puffed by Poe and Baudelaire, and so unclassical, dominates every page. The words are not odd, they are merely at times oddly related. Later, when Joyce evolved a composite language, it appeared to some people (like myself) more satisfying and logical than the jargon of 'Ulysses', because this new language has a recognizable basis in philology. In 'Ulysses' there are such elementary experiments as 'A screaming bittern's harsh high whistle shrieks. Groangrousegurgling Toft's cumbersome whirligig turns slowly the room right round-about the room'. This is simple, it reveals meaning, is emotionally apprehended. 'Steel shark stone onehandled Nelson, two trickies Frauenzimmer plumstained from pram falling bawling.' Though the words are simple, this is not easy. It is not readily apprehended either emotionally or by analysis. It lives only in its context. Such writing reveals in miniature the linguistic habits of Dylan Thomas.

His basic device (which Joyce later systematized) is the invention of words. This device is fully in accord with Dylan Thomas's own statement, 'Poetry is the rhythmic, inevitably narrative, movement from an overclothed blindness to a naked vision', and his definition of his poetic activity as '. . . the physical and mental task of constructing a formally watertight compartment of words, preferably with a main moving column' ('New Verse', October 1934). Dylan Thomas, in writing poetry, is not expressing so much as discovering his feelings. This is as it should be, for the reading and writing of poetry at any

DYLAN THOMAS

time are largely acts of discovery. The poet conventionally offers what he knows he has found, but Thomas offers the process of discovery itself. This unfinishedness is regarded by some as an insult to the reader, but in reality it is characteristic, honest, and one of the most attractive aspects of his work.

The invention of words, then, is inevitable in the expression of the half-perceived, incoherent sensations and ideas. And as his pen hovers between a host of choices, seeking some short-cut to expression as the Surrealists do by automatism, Dylan Thomas invents such terms as 'man-iron', 'bonerailed', 'seaspindle', 'seastruck', 'all-hollowed', 'pin-hilled', 'natron'. The presence of puns in these composites ('all-hollowed') indicates his pedantic dry humour. At other times, instead of fusing ideas together in this way, Thomas distorts their usual meanings, as in 'minstrel angle' (ministering angel?), 'triangle landscape' (here triangular+trinity, formed by the crosses of Christ and the robbers), 'ship-racked gospel', and the like. Real obscurity only starts when a false epithet is used, of which Joyce was rarely guilty. These are sometimes immensely expressive, as in 'dead nuisance' or 'iron mile', but the trick annoys when it hides rather than reveals meaning, as in 'colic season', 'cadaverous gravel', 'metal neptune'. This emotional use of epithet resembles fake-Surrealism. Real Surrealism is practically reached in his fourth trick: 'man of leaves', 'tree of nettles', 'wood of weathers', 'sixth of wind', 'house of bread'. This is very charming at first, but it bores by repetition. The final trick is the inaccurate use of verbs, which abounds in these poems in such lines as:

> Through the rampart of the sky
> Shall the star-flanked seed be riddled

> ('Poem 5')

Most of these verbal tricks are from time to time

completely successful and justified, as in the ten 'religious' sonnets in the 'Twenty-five Poems', where 'gallow grave', 'mountain minute', even 'glove of prints' and 'linen spirit' are impressive and logical in their context. At his best, Thomas reminds us of the Old Testament, James Joyce and Hopkins all at once. It matters little whether he reads them: his language partakes of all three.

In his later poems (since 1936) Thomas has diluted these verbal surprises. That his poems still startle our complacency is a proof that his first appeal was not due to mere bogus verbalism. It is well that he is losing some of these habits, which lead to preciousness of the most pompous kind. Not that it is to be despised, for preciousness itself can reveal a wealth of unsuspected fact. All poetry is precious.

III. *Biblical Symbolism*

I do not agree with a critic who said that there were two types of poems in the 1936 volume, 'sense' and 'nonsense' poems. The poems scarcely differ in method, and are made sensible by the pervading presence of the Bible and sexual symbolism.

Genesis, the Garden of Eden, the Fall, Adam, original sin, the presence of Cain, Job, Jacob, Abraham, Lazarus, the legends of Christ and Mary, form the bulk of the reference-matter, and even subject-matter of the 'Twenty-five Poems'. The fervency of these references is due to the fact that the Bible appears as a cruel and crazy legend, as seen through childish memories of hot-gospelling and the diabolical grimace of the Welsh Bethel. The Biblical element is further confused by a primitive metaphysics, related in the last analysis to a sexual interpretation of the universe:

Dawn breaks behind the eyes;
From poles of skull and toe the windy blood
Slides like a sea;
Nor fenced, nor staked, the gushers of the sky
Spout to the rod
Divining in a smile the oil of tears.
('Light breaks where no sun shines')

The philosophy is simple: the universe is sexually dynamic; bird, beast and stone share the same (sexual) life with man (an advance on the pretty pantheism of Wordsworth), but, for ever conscious of a sense of sin, Thomas conveys this as something terrible:

The horizontal cross-bones of Abaddon,
You by the cavern over the black stairs,
Rung bone and blade, the verticals of Adam,
And, manned by midnight, Jacob to the stars:
Hairs of your head, then said the hollow agent,
Are but the roots of nettles and of feathers
Over these groundworks thrusting through a pavement,
And hemlock-headed in the wood of weather.
('Poem 25': II)

Why horizontals and verticals (genitals would do)? The same arbitrary association links Abaddon, Jacob and Adam. Hollow agent (joke) is Death. Only 'cross-bones', 'cavern' and 'hemlock' produce horror. These lines form part of a sonnet relating growth from childhood to manhood. Death is present from beginning to end.

The 'horreur de la vie et l'extase de la vie' of Baudelaire are evenly balanced in Dylan Thomas. His universe is dynamic, frighteningly active and alive:

And now the horns of England, in the sound of shape,
Summon your snowy horsemen, and the four-stringed hill,
Over the sea-gut loudening, sets a rock alive;
Hurdles and duns and railings, as the boulders heave,
Crack like a spring in a vice, bone breaking April,
Spill the lank folly's hunter and the hard-held hope . . .
('Poem 10')

But, in consequence, death itself appears not as a negation, but as an equally dynamic force, as old as Adam:

> The wisemen tell me that the garden gods
> Twined good and evil on an eastern tree;
> And when the moon rose windily it was
> Black as the beast and paler than the cross.
>
> ('Poem 3')

Death, not life, is the measure of time:

> A worm tells summer better than the clock,
> The slug's a living calendar of days.   ('Poem 7')

So it is that the life-death problem in Dylan Thomas is as unresolved as the sex-sin problem. These dualisms are again related to a theological dualism, body-soul, as expressed in the first poem of the collection:

> I, in my intricate image, stride on two levels,
> Forged in man's minerals, the brassy orator
> Laying my ghost in metal,
> The scales of this twin world tread on the double,
> My half ghost in armour holds hard in death's corridor,
> To my man-iron sidle.   ('Poem 1')

This is more than lay philosophy, for it is implicit here that the triumph of the body is death of the spirit, since the 'man-iron' (flesh) and 'ghost in armour' (soul) are equally aggressive elements. It is only owing to this primitive interpretation that Thomas is able to confuse sexual and spiritual values in the ten 'religious' sonnets.

These so-called 'sonnets' (they are 14-line poems) cannot be considered separately, as together they form a unit ('Poem 25'). The technique is cumulative, impressionistic, though in one or two sonnets the subject is directly presented. Subjects, rather, for though the theme is the life-death antagonism, it is inextricably bound up with Old and New Testament mythology and sexual symbolism. It is rash to reduce such works to a formula, but for me they represent a double pattern of

Biblical and sexual imagery, the recognizable characters being Satan (identified with death and sin), sex (i.e. life, represented by Adam and even Gabriel), Mary (the justification of sex through child-bearing and suffering, but none the less a worldly symbol), and Christ (victim and blood-offering rather than hero).

Sonnet II, quoted above, expresses the identification of sex with sin and nature through Biblical reference. The third sonnet is confused, and in it the Old Testament wait for the Messiah, the Paschal Lamb, the three-days' death of Christ and the Ram of the Zodiac are so related that only the author could give a satisfactory explanation, if there is one. Not that it matters, for even a few lines of that poem should show Dylan Thomas's capacity for 'montage', as he works together a sense of time, the foreshadowed conflict of life and death principles, against a scriptural and sexual background:

> First there was the lamb on knocking knees
> And three dead seasons in a climbing grave
> That Adam's wether in the flock of horns,
> Butt of the tree-tailed worm that mounted Eve,
> Horned down with skullfoot and the skull of toes
> On thunderous pavements in the garden time.

Such verse is not intellectually rich, but sensually and emotionally it is profound. The fourth sonnet is a passage of sexual mysticism, in which love and sex are identified as a prelude to the nativity (Sonnets V and VI). 'And from the windy West came two-gunned Gabriel' (V). The narrative begins moving with this first line, the gangster-disguise of Gabriel (however naïve) giving the sense of shock and incredible difficulty by the Annunciation. Again cabbalistic tricks come to the aid of the poet, who conjures us a miracle with a pack of cards and a mumbo-jumbo of literary and Biblical allusion. Sonnet VI continues in the same vein, being a gruesome conception and nativity in one, contrived once more by a cabbalistic formula:

> He in a book of water tallow-eyed
> By lava's light split through the oyster vowels
> And burned sea-silence on a wick of words . . .

But this time the difficulties are not shirked, and all the horrors of birth (as suggested by Genesis and Milton perhaps) are conveyed in a brutally effective language:

> And love plucked out the stinging siren's eye,
> Old cock from nowheres lopped the minstrel tongue
> Till tallow I blew from the wax's tower
> The fats of midnight when the salt was singing;
> Adam, time's joker, on a witch of cardboard
> Spelt out the seven seas, an evil index,
> The bagpipe-breasted ladies in the deadweed
> Blew out the blood gauze through the wound of manwax.

The attending presence of the siren and cock (both symbolizing lust and sacrifice), Adam (the sinner), and the 'ladies in the deadweed' (again sirens, Fates, Furies, acting as midwives) heightens symbolically the horror of Christ's difficult, and indeed *unnatural*, birth. The next sonnet summarizes Christ's career: not the conventional tale so much as the bringing into focus of all Biblical legend, and a new identification of man with God and the universe. Its concentrated rhetoric—

> Now stamp the Lord's prayer on a grain of rice,
> A Bible-leaved of all the written woods,
> Strip to this tree: a rocking alphabet,
> Genesis in the root, the scarecrow word,
> And one light's language in the book of trees;
> Doom on deniers at the wind-turned statement—

brings together the literal fanatic, doubting Thomas and the twentieth-century modernist, while before them lies a world of living fact in which spiritual and physical realities meet.

The eighth sonnet, the Crucifixion, is the best.

This was the crucifixion on the mountain,
Time's nerve in vinegar, the gallow grave
As tarred with blood as the bright thorns I wept;
The world's my wound, God's Mary in her grief,
Bent like three trees and bird-papped through her shift,
With pins for teardrops in the long wound's woman.
This was the sky, Jack Christ, each minstrel angle
Drove in the heaven-driven of the nails
Till the three-coloured rainbow from my nipples
From pole to pole leapt round the snail-waked world.
I by the tree of thieves, all glory's sawbones
Unsex the skeleton this mountain minute,
And by this blowclock witness of the sun
Suffer the heaven's children through my heartbeat.

(To establish a hasty glossary, it seems evident that 'Time's nerve'=Christ, i.e. most sensitive point in history; 'gallow'=shallow+gallows; line 3: 'I'=Christ (if it means Dylan Thomas the poem loses); line 5, 'three trees'=crosses; 'bird-papped'=association of dove, also undeveloped, virginal; 'pins for teardrops'—compare Picasso's imagery, the very tears wound; 'Jack Christ'— Hopkinese, Christ is Everyman; 'minstrel angle'= ministering angel, also literally minstrel angle, that is each corner of the singing sky; 'heaven-driven'—the responsibility for the 'crime' rests with God, not man; 'three-coloured rainbow'—a new covenant made by the Trinity (see Milton); 'snail-waked'—snail symbol of destruction, sloth and lust; 'sawbones'—doctor; 'mountain'—gigantic, important; 'blowclock'—literally so, or the lifeless Christ's body become a symbol.)

In a sense this poem seems to symbolize the birth of love through the death of sex. Mary suffers the true punishment of Eve—not merely the pangs of child-birth, but the death of her offspring. The full symbolism only appears towards the end of the poem, with the words

'Unsex the skeleton this mountain minute'. A similar instance of sexual frustration occurs in 'I in my intricate image', in the words

> a cock on the dunghill
> Crying to Lazarus the morning is vanity.

The conclusion to be drawn from this fine crucifixion poem is disturbing. After presenting in all his poems a brilliant sexual interpretation of life, Dylan Thomas has here presented a sexual interpretation of death. The secret of death, and its horror, is that it is sexless. (Note: this may seem a far-fetched interpretation of a straight-forward poem. The answer is that all interpreting is dangerous, and never quite in focus. The poet is rarely entirely responsible for his implications, they rest with the reader.)

These poems owe their success to their density rather than to their outlook, though the outlook is original and stimulating. One or two of them are too exclusively montage, but as a whole they concentrate admirably in a final synthesis the tentative self-exploration of the rest of the volume.

In Dylan Thomas's later poems this Biblical back-ground narrows (some would say broadens) considerably. The 'Poem in October' ('The Year's Poetry', 1935) is a variation on the theme 'In the beginning was the Word', for in it all living things and natural objects are defined in terms of letters, vowels, syllables, etc. This poem could well have appeared nauseatingly literary, were it not for the fact that the subject is sustained by a strong sense of universal analogy, the one-ness of life, and justified by the poet's presence in the poem. This is a good instance of Thomas's pseudo-cabbalistic mystery, an effect which is readily obtained with few properties, but for a full development of which Thomas has not the necessary background. Let us remember (as a warning to school-girls who regard Dylan Thomas as a magician) that Professor Saurat once affirmed that Rimbaud's 'Les Voyelles' was based on the mysteries of the Cabbala. At seventeen, Rimbaud could easily obtain a smattering (about five lines) of knowledge of those mysteries from a Larousse dictionary. . . .

Towards 1937 Thomas broke slightly away from Biblical background, only to err consciously or unconsciously towards church ritual. This may have been due to Eliot or George Barker. That it was not successful can be seen in the poem 'It is the sinners' dust-tongued Bell claps me to churches' ('The Year's Poetry', 1937). Though there are some fine movements in the poem, in spite of the clarifying of the images the theme is less clear than in his earlier poems, and it leaves a sense of frustration. 'In Memory of Ann Jones' ('The Year's Poetry', 1938), which is perhaps his best poem since then, is funda-mentally religious, and is Biblical rather than church-going. Even the poem 'There was a Saviour' ('Horizon', May 1940) is only a new outlet for the Messianic legend, and the typical imagery is ritualistic.

It would be ridiculous to claim Thomas for any church. It is sufficient to note to what entirely different uses T. S. Eliot and Dylan Thomas have put the Bible for purposes of poetry. Thomas is much nearer Blake, one might even say nearer Donne, but also perilously near Rimbaud's 'Les Premières Communions'.

IV. *Sexual Symbolism*

'Poetry must drag further into the clear nakedness of light more even of the hidden causes than Freud could realize' (Dylan Thomas, 'New Verse', October 1934).

So wrote Dylan Thomas in his admission that he had

been influenced by Freud. The influence is first of all general, understandable in a poet whose chief pre-occupation is to explore childhood and adolescence. Only a reader of Freud can receive the full impact, which is enormous, of Dylan Thomas's predominantly sexual imagery. The influence of Freud would seem to go even farther (see p. 102) in view of the poet's acknowledgment that his activity as a poet is one of self-discovery rather than self-expression or even self-analysis. In their finished state the poems suggest that self-analysis could be undertaken by such a poet only by analysing what he had written. That is to say, they are not the product of analysis, but the very raw material for it. They are in the fullest sense documents: they are not intellectual or cerebral, but so spontaneous that the poet himself might well be amazed and bewildered in face of them.

The sexual symbolism in the poems seems to work largely as an assertion of sexuality, of the sexual basis of all thought and action. Secondly, the poems also contain some implied defences of this sexuality, justifications offered by the poet to society and to his own conscience. A little probing reveals not a liberated body but an obsessed mind (as in D. H. Lawrence):

> And I am dumb to tell the crooked rose
> My youth is bent by the same wintry fever.
> ('The force that through the green fuse')

Dylan Thomas's imagery is predominantly masculine, to the point of onanism and homosexuality. And although the male sexual images are bold, harsh and triumphant, there is a sense of impending tragedy and frustration.

> I see that from these boys shall men of nothing
> Stature by seedy shifting
> Or lame the air with leaping of its heats.

> I am the man your father was.
> We are the sons of flint and pitch.
> Oh see the poles are kissing as they cross.
>> ('Two' in 'New Verse', June 1934)

The male is constantly expressed, naturally, in heroic images, such as the tower, turret, tree, monster, crocodile, knight in armour, ghost, sailor, Jacob's ladder, skyscraper. But side by side with these are other equally male sex-images which carry also the idea of death and disgrace, such as the snake, the slug, the snail and the maggot:

> In old man's shank one-marrowed with my bone,
> And all the herrings smelling in the sea,
> I sit and watch the worm beneath my nail
> Wearing the quick away.
>> ('New Verse', August 1934)

It seems evident that Thomas's allegiance to Freud has not resulted, in his poems, in the cleansing of sexuality from the Old Testament sense of sin. Even the 'Paradise Regained' poem (as one might call the last of the sonnet-sequence) ends on a combined note of creation and destruction:

> Green as beginning, let the garden diving
> Soar, with its two bark towers, to that Day
> When the worm builds with the gold straws of venom
> My nest of mercies in the rude, red tree.

For the vision of the worm creating is only gained after the sexual immolation of the male (Christ):

> I by the tree of thieves, all glory's sawbones
> Unsex the skeleton this mountain minute,
> And by this blowcock witness of the sun
> Suffer the heaven's children through my heartbeat.

The words 'unsex the skeleton' are a good indication of Thomas's problem, the reconciling of the creative and destructive elements of sex. In view of the prevailing sense of sin, this suspicion that sex is not an end in itself, and that the ultimate objective is irremediably obscure, it must be concluded that the poet's interpretation of sex is still as close to the Old Testament as to the psychology of Freud. The Bible provides the mythology by which the problem can be raised to a high and universal plane, while Freud gives the impetus to what is perhaps the most overwhelming and poignant sexual imagery in modern poetry.

V. *Shape*

'The more subjective a poem, the clearer the narrative line' (Dylan Thomas, 'New Verse', October 1934). This is eminently satisfying if considered only in reference to Dylan Thomas himself. His poems are admittedly subjective, and their structure is remarkably simple. Not only is the 'main moving column' of words present; there is in consequence a strong core of subject round which the imagery is grouped. For this reason, although many people are dismayed by the accumulation of imagery and pseudo-imagery in the poems (for he is a spendthrift poet), the poems are far from being chaotic. Thomas's fundamental simplicity is shown in two of his finest poems, 'The hand that signed the paper felled a city' and 'The force that through the green fuse drives the flower'. These two poems reveal a classical ability to develop fully a simple subject. They alone would prove him a considerable poet. (After painting his complex portrait of Gertrude Stein, Picasso needed all his genius to draw like a child.)

In many poems the overlaying of images seems to go too far. That this is not a sign of weakness, however, and that Thomas still has (or had until recently) this basis of simplicity, is shown in what appears to me his best poem,

'In Memory of Ann Jones' (1938). The poem is planned in a manner worthy of Valéry himself, and a wealth of imagery subdued to the subject. There are four phases: the burial, the feast, the character and the homage. Tied images unite these phases, all of them relating to death, her home, her character. The poem is, in the poet's words, 'a monstrous thing blindly magnified out of praise'. Here Thomas achieves a concentration which is to be found in glimpses in his earlier poems:

> I know her scrubbed and sour simple hands
> Lie with religion in their cramp, her threadbare
> Whisper in a damp word, her wits drilled hollow,
> Her fist of a face died clenched in a round pain;
> And sculptured Ann is seventy years of stone. . . .

The typical furniture of her room, which appears early in the poem ('In a room with a stuffed fox and a stale fern'), serves as a dominant tied image, reappearing brilliantly at the end to drive home the idea that her love might even bring the dead to life:

> . . . until
> The stuffed lung of the fox twitch and cry Love
> And the strutting fern lay seeds on the black sill.

Dylan Thomas's poems are somewhat coarse-grained because of the profusion of imagery, most of it in overtones, grouped round the centre. But in the best poems, as in 'In Memory of Ann Jones', the magnifying habit scores heavily. In more recent poems there is less overlaying, and in 'There was a Saviour' there is evidence of a more refining process of selection.

VI

Technically, Dylan Thomas has achieved nothing new. His alliterative and inventive tricks are as old as poetry. His personal rhythms are not unusual when compared with those of Hopkins. He writes with equal ease in fixed and loose forms. His outstanding merit, when compared with the other young poets, is his rich vocabulary, his sensual appreciation of words, his intense persuasive idiom which reveals him as one who is reaching towards all that is most living in our language. In that respect he is an anachronism, for he has not abandoned the wealth of the past for the somewhat thin idiom of Hollywood and the Middlesex suburbs as many poets are doing.

Thomas is lacking in genuine humour, though he is humorous enough in everyday life. He displays in his writings, surely enough, the traditional Welsh easy flow of speech. But most of his jokes are either purely verbal, or sad and a little sinister. The characteristic tone of his poems is grave and depressing. There is sorrow in his wit, which is grim. This grimness is to be found also in his stories, such as 'The Burning Baby' and 'The School of Witches', where it reaches cruelty.

Dylan Thomas is fundamentally a poet of the feelings, and is not a visual poet. He does not see clearly, and consequently is a cuckoo in the nest of the 'New Verse' observation poets. His main object is to feel clearly, which he has not yet achieved:

> I have been told to reason by the heart,
> But heart, like head, leads helplessly. ('Poem 19')

He seeks the world in himself, and consequently his work is entirely autobiographical.

His future depends on an enlarging of his simple vision of the sexual basis of life, and it is to be hoped that he will not abandon his essential subject. That problem itself, and his evident conflict as to its solution, should provide him with an inexhaustible and vital theme. He is potentially the most modern of the young poets now writing, because of his assimilation of Joyce, Freud and the Bible, and because so far he has rejected the influence of the generation immediately preceding his own. He, like no young poet save perhaps George Barker and Ruthven Todd, is his own poet. Thomas is the most old-fashioned of his generation in his apparent separation of his poetry from his politics. This might yet prove valuable. Technically he has little to do save to give his verbal inventions a better grounding in reality and in philology, to concentrate even more on that 'main moving column', and to concede less to that delight in a grimace by which every poet is tempted.

August 1940.

GEORGE BARKER: A PURE POET

I. *Beginnings*

Wʜᴇɴ art critics were first confronted with the sensual paintings of Van Gogh, they could do little but complain of his drawing and perspective. Van Gogh is all sensation, and one has to accept his '*pure painting*' and refrain from asking for the accuracy of an Old Master. After such acceptance, one might even realize that some profound attitude to life is expressed in that lavish brushwork.

With regard to painting, the public has learnt that lesson, but it has not yet realized that a poetry can also be written which is predominantly sensational, the emotions existing raw and natural, almost in a pure state. That is why George Barker, for instance, though he has produced several books and been applauded in a narrow circle, does not seem to have penetrated to the general public. It must be admitted, however, that though his work has the freshness, the spontaneity and purity of a Van Gogh, he is also what the painter was not, an intellectual. And it is only when reason too strictly controls his emotional vision that his poems fail. He is, perhaps, a self-conscious Van Gogh.

At first reading, Barker annoys, for, like most poets of any worth, his faults are as glaring as his qualities. In the early poems there were innumerable miltonic latinisms and barbarisms, while he was so unsophisticated as to use such quaint words as 'hark' to set one's teeth on edge. At moments one was tempted to call him a pedant, though in reality he was incredibly naïve.

There is little need to dwell on Barker's earliest poems, especially since the best of the 'Thirty Preliminary Poems' (Parton Press, 1933) were later reprinted in the

118

'Poems' of 1935. He was capable of writing nonsense like

> Do I not see
> My analgesia
> Lies not in surcease
> Absolute end? ('Love Poem')

Very often he was carried away in a vortex of sound:

> Whose absolute dumbness circumscribed by sound
> Dumbfounds and profoundly confounds the boundary
> Of my sense. . . . ('On First Hearing Beethoven')

The 'Sequence of Ten Sonnets' (which might well, though they are less profound, be compared with Dylan Thomas's ten sonnets written not long after) are, above all, an essay in violence; it is the chaotic flood of the emotion which is evident rather than its quality. They are almost unquotable, unless it be for such lines as

> Turn your eyes rearward and watch not the flames
> No martyred city, no stricken walls, no upheaval's
> Death rattle, only the final ebb of decay
> Receding from beneath your proceeding feet;
> The sinews and tendons of your limbs are flames
> Your body a golden brand leading the way.

Some capacity for writing is emerging from so much slapdash impressionism. Feeling and sensation are distorted by abstractions and crude phrasing in these poems, which, though they contain the basic imagery and themes of Barker, serve largely as an outcry against adolescence and a breaking of inhibitions which are occasionally distressing to observe. The most important thing about this book is the fact that, at that date, a young poet could be so self-contained as to ignore the stifling but necessary influences of the Eliot and Auden generations.

In 1934, in the 'New Verse' enquiry, he identified poetry with 'spiritual unravelling', said he was 'extremely

sceptical of Freud', had no connection with any political
party or creed, and said: 'I feel myself very powerfully
conscious of the purely verbal origin of a poem; that the
impulse is "spontaneous" I suspect, but cannot verify.'
At the same time he reached a phase when he was
playing heavily with language, writing lines like 'Could
vagrant self detect correct direction' and passages
like

> A creation insulate
> From the corrosive breath
> Of death; prohibiting the
>
> Collision of internecine states
> As two elements conflagrate
> End in ashes, we emulate.

Pedantic, but also evidence of a certain word-curiosity
which was to bear fruit. These are about the worst lines
in his 'Poems' (1935). In most of these poems he was
laying on words as Van Gogh laid on paint, in thick
explosive masses. Any word would serve his purpose,
down to miltonisms such as 'rondure' and 'preparant',
and he would re-echo such gloomy puns as 'and him
I mourn from morn to morning'. Such things as these
allowed the sadism of the critics full scope. Only most
of them forgot to say why the poems were worth reading.
Not, I think, for the elegant exercise, 'The Amazons';
nor for 'Daedalus', though it has some attractive
passages; nor 'Luctus in Morte Infantis'; nor 'Wraith
Friend', 'Venerable All Hills' or 'Fistral Bay'. But
because of the mature concluding lines of 'The Amazons',
the moving last eight lines of 'Luctus', the last ten lines
which redeem the whole of 'Wraith Friend'. These
poems, peacocks whose beauty is all in their tail, reveal
Barker's strength and weakness: a certain slowness of
concentration, a lack of self-confidence perhaps, in the

first stages of a poem, with a gathering strength and full flowering towards the end.

The bulk of the 1935 poems are of high quality, especially the 'Narcissus' poems and a dozen others which are concerned with the main problem obsessing Barker: the nature of identity, that is, the same problem as obsessed Valéry in 'La Jeune Parque' and 'Le Cimetière Marin'.

In the 'Narcissus' poems the legend is placed in a modern setting and astutely worked out:

> Travelling through a fine evening in a car
> The attentive line of my own face was at intervals caught
> From the sunlight in outline—the chin's framed curve,
> Lips, jaw's asseveration—on the windscreen;
> The reproduction on, the reality through
> I now no longer wander wondering who.
>
> ('Narcissus, I'; also in 1933 volume)

There is good word-placing and emotional observation here, and the writing is a model of condensed movement, the general bewilderment of the preceding parts of the poem being concentrated in the interplay of 'wander wondering who'. The preciosity is justified and is of the best type of preciosity; that is to say, a play of ideas and not merely of words.

These poems are minutely, if emotionally, formed unities, though the subject develops with unexpectedly bold twists. In 'Narcissus, II' the subject is already more complex; the same problem of self-knowledge, but extended towards dualism and androgynism, themes cunningly brought together at the end by a man-shadow image. It is in this that the 'correct direction' line occurs, but the poem can stand it. 'Narcissus, III' is the most sensual and provocative of them all, and is as real in its intimate physical focus as 'Narcissus, I' is real in its

intellectual focus. It may be taken as a specimen of
Barker at his best in that period:

> Seven-ribbed Narcissus of my dream
> Embrace me with your floral arm,
> Render me with love insensible—
> Still I will seek your lips and seek
> Your overpowering to overpower,
> Our deformed amour to conform in sleep.
>
> Triple-lipped Apollo, I consign
> Your visitation to the night,
> When, amid cavernous mislove, your orbs
> Large with anticipate lust must diminish
> As, beneath my smothering embrace,
> The shocks your nine limbs striving to impart
> Shudder into the gentle heaving of sleeping.
>
> Horror of abhorrent presence, depart
> Down that appalling alley whence
> Gathering labyrinthine character from its kind
> You came. Forget to remember the ardour of our meeting
> As with passionate fear I clasped your animal head
> And hid my knees in the flowers of your bowels.

Barker is here somewhat Surrealist, but for me the
main impact of the poem is in the mingled sensation of
love and horror, a suggestion of struggle, and the way
form is imposed on a shapeless experience. Those
English poets who, at one time, read their Laforgue too
analytically and neglected Mallarmé and Valéry, were
much farther from Symbolism than Barker. His statement is implicit, the sensuality and suggestion dominate,
radiate the meaning. It is at once evident that he is an
original poet (that is to say a poet): 'floral arm' con-
centrates the metaphors of a few centuries into a brilliant
new image (compare Valéry's 'Bras de pierreries', which
has similar power); the vulgar English sense of the word
'amour' produces the desired revulsion; there is nothing
to be excused but 'orbs' and 'anticipate', which are offset

by the 'cavernous mislove', the skilful delay between 'whence . . . and . . . you came', the placing of the word 'animal' (compare again Valéry's 'Ton rêve animal'), which summarizes a half-mythological experience, leading to the muffled brutality of the last line. A poem nearer French Symbolism than anything since the early Yeats.

These three poems alone make the book worth having, but there are equally fine things in 'I am that land', 'The Land is yours', 'The Leaping Laughers' and 'The Crystal', and some poems on the personality problem such as 'I too will end', 'Lax though the longing may wear' and 'This Destination not to be read'. The only derivative poems are the slightly 1930–Auden 'Love Apart' and 'His Perennial'. Barker was also pre-occupied with the ideal-real problem which he was to develop in 'Janus', and at that time the idea 'no feeble dream is as good as to act' developed into a cult of energy with a materialist basis, fully expressed in a number of poems. The sonnet beginning

> I am that land surrounding sea
> And sky; the structure of my hand
> Spreads promontories, and the mountains of knees
> Penetrate the great clouds of your desire,

is a conceit sustained in the manner of Donne; it fulfils completely Eluard's conception of metaphors standing alone as complete poems. This poem and 'The Land is yours' have few rivals in the conceit type among Barker's generation. The paradox of many of Barker's poems is that, though individual lines are often lax, the general effect is strong and he has a great power of concentration on subject. 'I too will end' is a good instance of this: although the images of flowers, electricity and architecture seem incompatible, they are reconciled by the sweeping treatment. As a final instance, 'Lax though

the longing may wear' shows a good sense of formal
pattern, an intricate network of imagery borne on a sound
sustaining rhythm:

> Lax though the longing may wear, cannot be done.
> These are the words of always are your lips
> Your limbs and looks, manifesto of all time
> To men, whose best is this, which consummate form
> Circumscribes shows exhibits Time's foremost
> Making.   So show no apprehension of fading
> Down the years' falls, such descents for ghosts
> Imperfect in time.   You rise above eras' seas
> The spaceless gull, knowing no destination
> Other than love, and that home is my heart
> Rising and falling over Time's horizons
> Like suns.   Lax though the longing grow
> To go together, your form will flow alone
> Along the future waves, and be a guide.

Here two or three simple themes are inextricably woven
together, as similar themes in Mallarmé, not through any
mysterious 'alchemy', as the Symbolists would say, but
by a spontaneous development.   Such a poem, oblique
though it is, conveying an instantaneous complexity of
feelings, should need no explanation, since, though it is
compact, it is not difficult.   It illustrates another quality
of Barker's best work, a passionate gentleness of image
and rhythm, relieved at times by the darker side of a
nature which over-insists, as in 'circumscribes shows
exhibits'.   It is to Barker's credit that in 1935 as in 1933
his qualities, like his faults, were very much his own.

II. *Neo-Symbolism*

'Calamiterror' (1937) can be best understood if read
in conjunction with his remarkable prose-poems in
'Janus'.   There is no place to analyse 'Janus' here, but

a few parallel passages will help to summarize the development of a theme in 'Calamiterror':

> The first third of existence is spent acknowledging birth, in growing older: the second in suffering the contest for supremacy between birth and death: and the final third in the acknowledging the inevitable victory of the latter. ('Janus' 50, 1934)

> Between the ribs of the violent man
> Beats the red centre of the world of death.
>
> ('Calamiterror' 18)

> Out of what outer darkness is one born but that approaching darkness to which one must return? ('Janus' 34)

> Time like a mountain made of my own shadow
> Collapsing on me, buries me in my life.
> It is the future, undermined by present,
>   Falling appallingly backward. ('Calamiterror' 35)

> I am suspicious of living, and not of death. ('Janus' 17)

> Spreadeagled like the full-length mirror
> Pinioned like brilliant butterfly,
> Fixed through gold axle on the Ixion sky,
> I blaze in vacuum of being's horror.
>
> ('Calamiterror' 45)

> I have thought much of death, and much of love. But the latter is the greater, for it can motivate. That is the conclusion the earlier pages of this record have decided. I could not die, for death's sake, but must, for love's.
> ('Janus' 40)

> Continually the women weeping in Irun's ruins
> Call in distress with voices like swans;
> I hear that cry which breaks the womb or room
> Wherever I stand, and forces me to go.
> ('Calamiterror' 49)

'Calamiterror' at once roused the admiration of the critics, in spite of certain obvious defects. There is a great deal of repetition, especially in the first half of the book, where a long series of questions are followed by sequences of answers, all asking and answering almost the same things. The imagery itself is limited and repetitive, while the stanza soon becomes monotonous until the line fills out towards the end of the poem. These defects are inherent in the method, which pertains less to poetry than to music and painting. It is what one might call a symphonic poem, the theme being constantly restated and elements of it developed and embroidered until the poem becomes an intricate network of tied imagery. Or at times one has the impression of the poet exploiting every implication of his imagery, as a painter making a picture out of a variation on one colour. Most of the book is well out of the main current of English poetry in the 'thirties, being in method closer to the technique of the Symbolists or to certain aspects of Eliot.

It would be impossible to summarize the 'argument' of such a poem, for its power is not in the argument but in its rich interplay of feeling and image. It can be read as a sort of imaginative autobiography, a struggle from darkness to the light, a development from self-interested pessimism and suicide-impulse to the equation of himself with (as in one of his later poems) 'the mass of man'. At some points one is torn between comparing Barker with Blake or with Dylan Thomas, in his Swedenborgian treatment of birth for instance:

> Time is dark, and in the centre burns
> The babe with salamander on his breast;
> The salamander is species of the sun,
> Whose clouds are horror, fear and decay.
> The babe is universe with hands and feet of stars,
> His blood is gravitation running real. . . .

The comparison with Thomas would be false, because, though they are equally 'sensational' poets, Barker is

more selective and his vocabulary and texture are more
refined. Sometimes, however, he resembles Thomas
closely, in such lines as

> My winter woman of margarine and tears,

or:

> I tear my guts out on the platform
> Or rummage in my stomach with bloody hands.

The first few parts of the poem deal largely with the
birth-death theme, but in Book V it emerges from
principles to facts ('By the Babylonian stream I meant
Ealing'); then, after some strange visions of Milton and
Blake, after which the poet suddenly becomes apocalyptic
and beholds the chaos of the modern world, the subject
develops into an intense personal struggle. Book VI,
the crisis, contains the best verse description of the
'between two wars' period that has been written, showing
the individual caught in a loop of circumstance, and
explaining, three years before the invasion of Poland, why
poets can no longer exist in Europe. The book then
works towards an immense deliverance, a delivery, as it
were, from the womb of self into a universal sympathy,
in a rising feeling and rhythm for which Barker's peculiar
experiments as a poet had already prepared him:

> I remember again the three women weeping on Irun's ruins
> Whose tears will wash the Rhone and Rhine and whose grief
> Thrust up like crystal towers the architecture of Time.
> I see England
> With the underground mines run bleeding along her like
> > wounds.
> I hear the great Lancastrian shafts delivering sounds
> Of sorrow and appeal, or watch the falling stacks
> Like hands for charity, or fallen, clenched.

'Calamiterror', with all its faults, is perhaps the most
successful long poem of the 'thirties. Its complicated
technique and development show that the direct manner

favoured then by poets was not necessarily the most modern or the best. At the same time, Barker's development in the poem, from depth to breadth, from personal to public feeling, from overlaid imagery to a startling clarity of language, assured him some future as a poet and a high place among the poets of his own generation. The 'thirties produced a large body of political poetry, much of it infused with a broad imaginative vision and a grasp of human problems. Of all the poems bearing on the Spanish war, Barker's poem will stand with the highest, next to Auden's 'Spain' and not below it.

III. *Directions*

Since 1937 Barker has fulfilled his promise, and there is little need to insist on the virtues of his last book, 'Lament and Triumph', 1940. The long 'View of England' could be interestingly compared with Prokosch's eight-page 'Ode' and Allott's 'Men Walk Upright', both of 1938. If in its total effect it is not superior to them, it has incidental beauties which set it apart. Its total effect is diminished only because Barker seemed unable to grasp the spirit of the places he mentioned. At a time when Grigson and Auden excelled at grasping the meaning of places, the one by detailed observation and the other by instinctive generalization, this defect in Barker seemed the more noticeable. His inability in this direction had been evident in 'Northumberland' ('Poems'), which, as a Northerner, left me cold. One or two places are well presented, however, for instance:

> There's nothing here but the mere loneliness
> Of the long lost Gothic ache to heaven;
> Like the lily in which the dead dress
> Salisbury is a beautiful funeral.

Barker's romantic imagination works in its usual way,

filling out the poem with some brilliant pageantry. But at its best the emotion penetrates his broad perceptions and emphasizes the rhythm:

> But beside Windermere I shall move at night
> When the West Wind blows into my window
> The tresses of Venus where they wave their light,
> Even though I come from a dream of splendour.
>
> Not less strong than the indomitable rock,
> Not less lovely than the lake and the star,
> The wife of England roves in the North,
> Among the derelict cities and the memories of war.

If most of these poems reveal a new attitude to language in Barker, there is still little change in his method of conveying sensation in memorable terms; he writes of rain falling:

> Then at my face the shower of rain
> Stardusts me with a handful of its brilliants,
> Flecking my lashes like worlds: the violence
> Of winds may shake them, but only fall for pain.
>
> > ('Triumphal Ode')

It is this same sensual quality which makes of all Barker's 'political' poems something far more than political poems in the usual sense of the term. This can be seen to the full in a few lines of his 'Elegy on Spain', which, although they are immediately accessible, have all the sensuousness and eloquence of his earlier work:

> Can the bird cry or any word on the branch
> That blanches at the bomb's red wink and roar,
> Or the tall daffodil, trodden under the wheel of war,
> But spring up again in the Spring for it will not stay under?
> Thunder and Mussolini cannot forbid to sing and spring
> The bird with a word of determination, or a blossom of hope,
> Heard in a dream, or blooming down Time's slope.

The Elegies and Epistles in his book also show that this quality remains undiminished. It is almost irrelevant

E

to congratulate Barker on his new purity of language and his 'New Verse' attempts at reporting the external world: by far the most important thing that has happened is that he has remained an individualist in spite of all his concessions to fashion, and that the sensual power of his poems is undamaged. This can be seen quite well in the 'Seven Pacific Sonnets' published in 'Horizon' (November 1940), although the direct method of address diminishes his scope. It is a far cry from the involved harmonies of the obsessed Narcissus to this direct expression of the meaning of war, but although the thought is now clearer and less wrapped in imagery, the same Barker of the early poems is there, in such lines as

> Out of the bogus glory and the synthetic hate,
> The welter of nations and the speeches, O step down,
> You corpse in the gold and blue, out of a cloud,
> My dragon fly, step down into your own:
> The ditch and the dislocated wings and the cold
> Kiss of the not to be monumental stone.

The abdication is from Europe, but not from poetry.

December 1940.

JULIAN SYMONS: THE CRITIC AS POET

I

SURREALISM, the spontaneity of Dylan Thomas, the Left propaganda and music-hall aspects of Auden, are the most dangerous reefs for the younger poets at the present time, being methods easily adopted but liable to stunt a follower's own gifts if he has any. In the face of these dangers it is reassuring to find stabilizing, though experimental, elements in many of the new poets, including Allott, Symons and Ruthven Todd. There are one or two others who are also effectively applying a brake to eccentricity, for instance R. B. Fuller, who still has much to learn from Robert Graves, and D. S. Savage, who runs the risk of becoming academic through a too rigid adherence to the attitudes of Yeats.

Julian Symons is an interesting subject, because not only has he never hesitated to express his opinions, so that it is clear enough where he stands, but because he successfully edited his own magazine, 'Twentieth Century Verse', and did much to encourage talent which could find little expression elsewhere. The very time of the birth of his magazine is not a bad clue to its editor: it appeared when 'New Verse' was becoming doctrinal, and was in at the death of that amusing Surrealist and Communist adventure 'Contemporary Poetry and Prose'. The direct ancestor of 'Twentieth Century Verse' was no doubt 'New Verse', but in Symons's fathering of so many of the younger poets he is no doubt hatching a dangerous brood which might do more than continue what 'New Verse' stood for. For the Grigson group hardly realizes yet that it is being followed by an equally intelligent, equally pugnacious and equally discontented generation.

II. *Views*

In an article on Hart Crane ('Twentieth Century Verse', No. 8) Julian Symons made one of those inclusive statements which are so easily turned against poets later in their career:

(1) Art is to the artist an autobiographical game, disguised or honest.

(2) Poetic sensitiveness is the poet's rationalization of the interplay between possible and actual, wish and event: its usefulness is limited and it is the cause of most bad verse.

(3) The poet is, or ought to be, the perfect unconscious 'mass-observer': a mass in one. It follows that he is also a very good case for mass-observation.

(4) In poetry the factual is to be preferred to the abstract, words to music, the real to the ideal. Poetry creates legend, and that is generally a good thing: for the poet to live inside his own legend is almost always a bad thing.

(5) Poetry has social value: but his own poetry should have no social value to a poet.

It is a rare thing to find a poet whose criticism and verse are not in some ways at variance, but Symons's 'Confusions about X' are, as poems, almost a rigorous demonstration of the few points (which I number for convenience) quoted above. And that is a tribute to his poems, since the points, save for one or two minor objections, are good. The sometimes incoherent theme

[Photo Basil Shackleton, A.R.P.S., F.I.B.P.

JULIAN SYMONS

of his book is a psychological self-pursuit, a decidedly 'autobiographical game'. The statement is a challenge to all those who write no verse of their own to speak of, to the Boileaus who tell the Racines and Molières that they should be more 'objective'. Dramatic poetry is perhaps the only pseudo-escape from autobiography, though the typical dramatic poetry of our time, Eliot's and Auden's, is frankly autobiographical. In a sense, autobiographical restrictions are the only guide to real objectiveness: the poet who ranges beyond his own experience is asking for trouble.

'Poetic sensitiveness': here Symons seems to agree with Grigson, but even more so with Laura Riding (who once wrote to me in almost the same terms: 'You have a delicate and agile faculty, attention to things, which you allow to run loose and split up your poetic energy into freakish and sometimes absurd verbal minutiae': a statement which the young Surrealist then found shocking, only to learn by experience that it was quite true, and true of too much modern poetry). Symons here defends the integrity of the poem against indiscriminate gush, and perhaps, also, against Surrealism. Surrealism, however, is good enough in its right place and time. The word 'sensitiveness' is not well used here: 'suggestibility' would be better.

'The perfect unconscious mass-observer.' The word 'unconscious' is most apt here: it puts the 'reporting' urge in a more acceptable light than 'New Verse' has yet done. It leaves room for Thomas and Barker, for instance.

Paragraph four again emphasizes Symons's adherence to both Grigson's and Laura Riding's business-like approach to poems. It is (like theirs) his justification as an editor. Only the first part of the last statement is acceptable: as for the second part, the poet's poems are his sole justification of his rôle in society, so they must have value for him; and since, through them, he shapes and discovers his conception of life and society, the poems should be as important to him as a state-controlled newspaper is to the state.   Symons is right enough in its application to in-breeding literary poets.

III. *An Autobiographical Game*

'Confusions about X', Symons's first volume, is, then, an autobiographical game, a serious and amusing game. Not content with dualism, in the manner of Freud he divides himself into three parts at least, the editor keeping a careful watch over his personalities in the manner of Baudelaire or a Chinese box.   These figure in the 'Prologue to a Sonnet-Sequence' as an aggressor (successful man of the world?), a brooder (destructive poet, critic and revolutionary), and 'your humble', a capable Cockney umpire.   These sonnets are as provocative as the first line, 'My joking two now bow: honours are even', but they exist mainly as a statement of the problem, which is never solved.   It should be said at once that in this form the problem does not entirely dominate Symons's book (as similar problems dominate the entire work of Dylan Thomas), so that the term 'Confusions' is appropriate.   We agree with the author:

X is getting roaring drunk on my Imperial Tokay
X is smashing up the flat, his ham-fists crashing through
    wood.
I should like to know more about X.

X is sometimes even more sinister than this:

        Where is that demon who is born of night,
        The gull of death without his crying talons?
        His hurdy gurdy over years of light

Wheels with its taut embracing columns.
He is the X to whom I play the drums
Through dutiful quiet rooms;

He is the winding music that I choose,
My ravelled sleeve, my polyphonic wrongs,
The black to-morrow that I never play;
Music in death and man as I go round
Is hidden in the pier or a sea-wind
Has borne it idly home.   ('Musical Box Poem')

Actually the best part of this poem is the final two stanzas,
which cannot be quoted here: the above is merely an
instance of how the X theme emerges at unexpected
moments, X being a mysterious quantity, like Eliot's
sinister 'silent man in mocha brown', and equally amusing
in spite of (or because of?) the poet's continual mental
reservation, by which he probably means that X=O.
The main point for the moment is that X is a square peg
in a round hole: X is dissatisfied, X is a worried
intellectual craving for a world of simpler values:

(Let the ambiguous heart accept whatever may happen
As the child accepts the witches in the wood
And the other tales where everyone is good
Let us accept hate as being in the pattern;

and, finally, X is that suicide impulse already seen in the
'Musical Box Poem', and seen even better in 'On
Liberals, 1938':

And your world ends suddenly like torn silk
You tear the mirror in pieces like tearing silk
For time is up you have upset the table
Time is up, your red trousers are burnt
Time is up the wireless is smashed
O helpless now O see

This is reality.

It is a little inaccurate to say that X equals nothing:

it might be better said that X wants to become something, but could only do so by immersion in a group; by a simplification of loyalties. Seeing Symons's problem this way I no longer find it trivial, as it could have been: it is essentially the problem that made so vital the early poems of Romains, and the 'Salavin' novels of Duhamel.

But it should not be thought that this psychological problem limits the scope of the poet: one of the interesting things about it is to observe the method by which the obsession can be introduced without standardizing the poems. A good instance of this is the 'Poem for a Birthday', especially in its concluding lines, which demonstrate Symons's technical maturity better than the poems already quoted:

> . . . No angel knows a face
> Or knows a face's X,
> Or synthesizes why
> This year's corollaries
> Are the unvarying stories
> Of the dramatic truces
> And the possible eyes.
>
> In your beginning year
> I cannot wish you more
> Than could the savage angel.
> But give to you alone
> Whatever may be good,
> The power within the wood
> To walk unharmed or moved,
> Look guilelessly on summer.
> What is not in myself,
> What I shall never be,
> The island, the real tree,
> I wish you now, to go
> Scatheless among all eyes,
> Unpeopling desire,
> And fishing by the weir
> When papers announce war,

That looking at the sane
You finally resign,
While they are counting ten
Be stressed and single, one.

The imagery of the first part here is specialized and can be followed only in reference to what had preceded it. But after the last movement, which has great tenderness, Symons cannot be dismissed (as Romains was) as a cerebral poet. Yet, apart from the angel, whose function is not clear, precision is achieved by an accumulation of facts and actions rather than sentiments and words. As for the technique, Auden has passed by: the delicate, intricate Auden of the 1930 poems. But it is noticeable that Symons has had the good sense to assimilate a method (and one which he practises several times with great success in this book) without assimilating the personal attitudes and mannerisms which accompanied it, so that he is not an imitative poet. The opposite would apply to most followers of Auden, especially to Gavin Ewart. As for maturity, its proof is in the slow, controlled movement, which is difficult to achieve in such short lines, which lend themselves to rapid, breathless movement. This slowness is gained by successive reflections, marked by strong pauses, and brought together by the skilful placing of 'I wish you now', which prepares a new 'return' or rehandling of the subject—a trick which few modern poets have fully mastered. The final word is a return to the poet's problem of one-ness. The placing of this word is again very cunning, taking one back to the X in the middle of the poem.

IV. *Evasions*

Since the war of 1914-1918 English poets have been more outspoken on political matters than ever before, and enthusiasts have even gone so far as to speak of 'Left' and 'Right' poetry, refusing to read Roy Campbell or Auden according to their own political sympathies. That is a mistake, for although there is much that is ephemeral in the present tendency, and though poetry often suffers by being too topical, the historian of the future will be obliged to admit this as an age of highly accomplished political poetry. That it is not exclusively so proves that the poets have enlarged the scope of poetry without endangering poetry or reducing it to pamphlet level. There are many subtle ways of political expression : the greatest of them, and one in which Byron and Browning led the way, is in using the whole arsenal of language, down to the imagery of kitchen utensils (which Baudelaire himself did not despise), until poetry, if it is not written by all, is accessible to all.

Julian Symons, as an intellectual, might well have remained outside in political matters, but his poems are proof that he cannot do so. The plunge, as seen in the first poem, 'Dedication', is deeper than one expected :

> And horror begins now, it is with horror I see
> All your faces are like mine, you are
> Puppets like me in the iron fist of money,
> Taking the financier's heavy downward step.
> This time expanding is my demon Time,
> My horror sea where no one ever is
> But the endless man who is afraid to weep.

But in spite of this commitment, Symons is no nearer a party, no nearer one-ness, than Allott was in his 'Men Walk Upright'. The split-man has a foot in both camps still :

> Figuratively I am still with you, I am the epicure and
>   appreciator of cigars,
> Collector of snuff-boxes, wearer of black tie . . . etc.

Like the psychological theme, the political theme is not

fully worked out in this volume, but there are two fine poems, among the best, in which this 'Dedication' is amplified. One of them is the 'Garden Poem', which is a confession of a disillusioned intellectual. The attitude is one of mental revolt inhibited by practical impotence; revolt in

> Looking in childhood through uncandid eyes
> I saw without emotion and without surprise
> The splendid and remote ideal
> Not wished, the shabby and the real
> Accepted, the commonplace preferred to the wise.

impotence in

> Too late now the uncomplicated faith,
> The raised-fist marching and the missionary death,
> The accurate scientist straight as a crow
> Cutting a path through rock or snow,
> The wonderful illusion or the simple life.
>
> For the sensitive heart and the cultivated mind
> Knew the fairy tale is falsehood but will never lift the
>   blind;
> To us, the sceptical and calm,
> The dream is final, and we come
> To face the deadly face in a hostile land.

But at the same time Symons seems to have joined at least the ranks of quietism and passive resistance:

> Yours is not my world then, I shall be in opposition
> To the gay recruiting singing and the barked decision.

The poet, then, retires into his job of poetry, observing and preserving:

> What an eye can see and a brain record
> And a hand put down in a halting word,
> Sitting in the garden I can offer you now.

That is how it should have been, had not the crisis of 1938

shown (see 'On Liberals, 1938') that there was no longer anything worthy to be preserved:

> You should know that the coloured mountains are merely a backcloth,
> The stuffed countryside is dead, however lifelike.

To abandon strict neutrality for the moment, it is hard to accept the stiffening of this hands-off attitude as the present war developed. In one of his poems, written presumably at the outbreak of war, Symons concluded:

> The houses are shut and the people go home, we are left in
> Our islands of pain, the clocks start to move and the powerful
> To act, there is nothing now, nothing at all
> To be done: for the trouble is real: and the verdict is final
> Against us. The clocks go round faster and faster. And fast as confetti
> The days are beginning to fall.   ('Pub')

Now this is admirably written with a dying fall, but the sentiments are those of a dying generation: in fact, they are the sentiments, which are not without grandeur, of Eliot's 'East Coker'. The critic might reply that there is a great deal to be done, and which poets can do, instead of abandoning very serious responsibilities. Walking out of the past is not a very sure way of walking into a future. Symons, as most writers are tempted to do, conceives of a narrower set of responsibilities than those of a citizen, and has since written:

> Finally, one can only repeat generalizations. The poet, *in society as it is now constituted*, has no 'duty'; the poet is not of necessity concerned with the alteration of society; he may accept or reject or remain indifferent to the effects of war. Where there is no doctrine there can be no rules. He must accept his position, and make the best of it. He must try to preserve his individual integrity, to increase his technical skill. To move continually from obscurity to lucidity, from ignorance to knowledge, from confusion to

harmony: that, to-day as in the last three hundred years, is the *poet's* only problem. ('Now', June-July 1940, No. 2)

To which a critic with a broader conception of a poet could reply: 'You alienate the poet from his physical environment: he is also a man and a member of *society as it is now constituted*, and, like other members, has some power to determine its nature. There is something to be said for Lautréamont's "The poet should be the most useful member of his tribe." The poet is not merely an onanist or an amuser: he is (at the risk of being Shelleyan) the very *conscience* of society. Maybe he has no direct *duty* concerning bloodshed and legislation, but he has a duty at least to himself, the preservation and creation of values which make war impossible and sanity possible. He must accept this position, which is the only one in which he can hope to exist, the only one in which he can decently preserve his integrity. Who, better than the poet, can lead the way from the obscurity of war to what should be the lucidity of peace? The poet's problem is to write poetry: like any bird laying an egg, he cannot remain indifferent to the conditions which affect his ability to do so. There are other things than stocks and shares in the making of a new order.' [1]

Such a reply, of course, would not be adequate, for it ignores the fact that in expressing his attitudes in prose or verse, as Symons has done, he is filling his place in

[1] Since writing the above, I find that Mr Harold Laski has expressed the point with greater force : ' The main body of our literature, like that of eighteenth-century France, is almost wholly, in its serious manifestation, one of criticism and dissent ; and if it be said that there are few men of letters with a positive faith to offer, that does not lessen the importance of the fact that their emphasis is essentially negation.' (In ' Where do we Go from Here ? ', Penguin.) I would add that there is a difference between the art-for-art's-sake negation of the nineteenth century and what might be called the positive negation of our time : we can no longer pretend that the social problems do not exist and that they do not affect the poet.

society as he ought to do: the theory is wanting, but the practice is right. Fundamentally the poet's problem in war-time is one of conflicting loyalties, and is almost the same as that of the craftsman driven into the infantry, or the husband and father cooped in a tank. Where the poets are mistaken is in socially underestimating their poetry: they should make it clear that, singly or as a body, they are fitted to do all that is beyond the power of any Ministry of Information, whether destructively or constructively.

V. *False Economy?*

Of the new poets, the strongest in formal quality are without doubt Allott, Symons, and perhaps Dylan Thomas in his peculiar way. Allott's formal strength is partly literary and historical, rather than a psychological necessity: he inherits certain restrictions from the Meta-physicals but has learnt a variety of tone comparable with that of Macneice. Almost the same applies to Symons, though his colloquial range is wider: his self-conscious control is at once psychological and, as it were, editorial, varying between types of poems. The idiom changes rapidly as X breaks furniture or listens to music or meditates by the sea.

Symons's poetry is economical, despite an occasional use of 'lists'. There is no overflow either of imagery or emotion. Sometimes, as in 'Colour Absent', the writing is thin:

> As, madly, talk of days to hide our fear
> Of night: as the applauding big-eyed children
> Clap hands to hide a terror, knowing when
> They're older there will be no power in terror.

The tightness (suppression of pronouns, etc.) is dissipated

by the repetition of 'terror', giving an impression of emptiness: a habit, incidentally, already overworked by Spender.

This economy is disastrous in such poems as 'This Year' and 'About Streets' with their unconvincing abstractions (these abstractions, which theoretically have a wide range, are in practice less effective than naming definite objects):

> If knowing every harmer
> Made simple to be happy
> Who would have need to fear
> The coming on-rush
> The resistless invasion
> The amazing vision
> The detective session
>
> The untenable position
> The deduced action
> 'Begun: finished'
> Or body's persuasion
> In normal town?

But this falls far below the active, visual idiom of his best poems. Symons has been reproved for such lines as 'Charming and useless as a girl's silk leg'. Take it or leave it, such a line is a clue to the stable element in Symons's imagery, which is, at its best, a human imagery. He is best in speaking of 'water slapping the sky', or 'From a plurality of evenings like hair and hands', or 'The childish darkness that fell down long ago'. The strongest criticism that can be made is that sometimes he forgets this, and that many poems are neither sensual nor sensuous enough.

Symons is an intellectual, and he is at his best when his intellect works on a problem which he feels acutely. This happens in one of his sonnets (like Thomas, he has developed the sonnet in a loose twentieth-century manner) where his intellectual vision results in a perfectly balanced and felt conceit:

> Amazement, not knowing where to begin,
> If the poor are cold or the warm are warm,
> Or the pectoral muscle or the abrogated sin,
> Or who was reckless and came to harm:
> You are the reckless, who are on the rim
> Of the world, travelling round and round
> Through sight, through black, through absence, through
>   ground,
> Who are in the centre, in the same place, and so see every-
>   thing dim.
>
> Outside there is nothing to be seen, nothing, nothing
> But the black of people and the black days rushing.
> To be in the centre, that is to wear a shape
> Centrifugal, so that warm is never enough,
> It is to wear amazement that the poor are happy, that
> Perimeter's in the centre, and that centre's not smooth but
>   rough.

Apart from questions of language, this ability so to develop a theme is the ultimate quality we have the right to demand of a poet. Symons has this (see also 'The River') quality for lack of which many young poets are now hopelessly floundering. The presence of this ability, even though he has exploited it only in a minor way up till now, is Symons's surest claim to the reading public's attention in the next few years.

October 1940.

WHAT ABOUT SURREALISM?

It is important to notice that no strong irrational conception of life and poetry arose in Britain after the Great War, as it did in Europe. Dadaism and Surrealism were produced by a disgusted and disillusioned Continent, and flourished especially in Germany and France. These movements are signs of a psychological illness in society, resulting from the horrors and irrationalism of war. If there was nothing more irrational in Britain than the new sexual-emotional doctrine of Lawrence (with a self-made psychology and personal 'philosophy'), the ghosts and dragons of Robert Graves, author of 'Poetic Unreason', and the fantasy-life of the Sitwells, that was because the worst effects of the war were less felt, or at any rate less articulate, than in other countries. Nothing comparable with Surrealism in this country emerged until after the great financial crisis of 1931, which profoundly moved the younger generation, who began to look about them, and, seeing the two million unemployed and the rapid disintegration of the European system, sought a cure in Marxism and Fascism, or an escape in Surrealism. So, paradoxically, Dadaism and Surrealism, which appear completely anti-intellectual, completely insane, were methods of preserving sanity, and even certain intellectual values, by affording an easy release into a world of make-believe. And something similar will happen after this war unless some sort of rational *modus-vivendi* can be achieved to make Europe worth living in.

If Dada claimed to be completely negative, and was mistaken, so Surrealism claimed to be completely positive, and was mistaken. Surrealism seemed at first, in the hands of Breton, Eluard, Aragon, Crevel and others, to refute any materialist conception of life. There were various 'periods' of Surrealism, each more mysterious than the last: the hypnotic period, the period of hallucinations, the period of accidents and found-objects, the anti-aesthetic period in which the only standards were subjective, or the manifestation of the extraordinary in all walks of life. We have to go back to Nerval's defence of madness, Rimbaud's confusion of the senses, the paranoia of Lautréamont (who was a forerunner of Kafka) and the alcoholism of Jarry, and roll them all into one, with a little admixture of the Marquis de Sade, Byron and Melmoth, to find anything like Surrealism in previous literature. Then Surrealism became finally pseudo-scientific. Breton had been a doctor: his followers adopted Freud (much against his will, for he wrote a letter of protest to the review 'Le Surréalisme au Service de la Révolution') and psycho-analysis, and claimed that Surrealism had above all an experimental and clinical value (as it has). They also adopted Marx and Engels, but hardly M. Stalin, and asserted that by spiritual means they would achieve the liberation of the human mind, the demolition of the bourgeois mentality, by upsetting all preconceived capitalist ideas of the world, thus hastening the progress to the ideal communist state of life. This may sound a travesty: it is, in a sense, for it is true that Surrealism, if wisely practised by a writer, can be the best method yet invented for breaking down those inhibitions which often prevent writers from achieving self-mastery and self-understanding. And it must be acknowledged that Surrealism has not prevented such men as Paul Eluard from writing really excellent work which can compete with anything their contemporaries have produced.

I think I am right in saying that until about 1930

Surrealism had received but scant, or derisory, attention in this country. It was my own generation, nourished on Freud and Marx, and heartily dissatisfied with the state of modern life, who took the plunge, backed by some sympathetic writers of the older generation, especially Herbert Read.

In 1936 Roger Roughton founded the only successful Surrealist review that has appeared in England, 'Contemporary Poetry and Prose'. Produced at his own expense, it ran for eighteen months, during which time ten numbers appeared. In about the same year appeared David Gascoyne's 'Short Survey of Surrealism', a rather scrappy book, but one which attracted some attention, partly because of the extraordinary anecdotes it contained, partly because of the excellent plates, and partly owing to the interesting translations of Surrealist poetry by various authors. Not long afterwards, a Surrealist group was formed in England, and a successful Surrealist Exhibition was held in London in 1936. It was amusing to watch the hypocritically scandalized reactions of the popular dailies: one of them had an article headed 'A Shocking Art Show: Girl Subjects of Surrealist Paintings'. The writer of the article, Pierre Jeannerat, expressed himself in the most violent terms: 'Decadence and unhealthiness of mind and body, the unleashing of low and abnormal instincts, a total lack of reason and balance, a distasteful revelation of subconscious thought and desires . . . these words are not too strong for some exhibits. As regards technique, it has to be admitted that the works show considerable ability.' After describing the shocked reaction of 'gentle, bewildered old women' (why did they ever leave home?) and the action of the Customs authorities in refusing to allow some of the exhibits to reach England, he advised the Government (which was then in the innocent hands of Mr Baldwin) to step in and 'ruthlessly tear several pictures from the walls'. The climax of the article was reached in the words 'But not only is much of Surrealism, as expressed at the exhibition, morbid and disgusting; it is also dull, so dull that it is worse than dead; it has already reached the stage of putrefaction.' So much for the 'Daily Mail': it is certain, however, that this was the best form of advertisement the exhibition could have had in this country. But Surrealism rapidly advanced to its academic stage in Britain, and was not really absorbed. The symposium on Surrealism by Herbert Read, Eluard, Breton, Davies and Hugnet, with its excellent illustrations, placed the debate on a more serious level.

Anyone interested in the manifestations of Surrealism among the younger poets of the 'thirties cannot do better than to look through the ten numbers of 'Contemporary Poetry and Prose', if he can obtain them. The first number started off mildly enough, though it contained Dylan Thomas's first Surrealist story, 'The Burning Baby', a strange tale of incest which, in its peculiar style, re-creates the fanatic atmosphere of his poetry in the very first lines:

> They said that Rhys was burning his baby when a gorse bush broke into fire on the summit of the hill. The baby, burning merrily, assumed to them the sad white features and the rickety limbs of the vicar's burning baby. What the wind had not blown away of the baby's ashes, Rhys had sealed in a stone jar. With his own dust lay the baby's dust, and near him the dust of his daughter in a coffin of white wood.
>
> They heard his son howl in the wind. They saw him walking over the hill, holding a dead animal up to the light of the stars. They saw him in the valley shadows as he moved, with the motion of a man cutting wheat, over the brows of the fields. In a sanatorium he coughed his lung into a basin, stirring his fingers delightedly in the blood. What moved with invisible scythe through the

valley was a shadow and a handful of shadows cast by the
grave sun.

The bush burned out, and the face of the baby fell away
with the smoking leaves.

This writing is much less concentrated than Thomas's
poems, and I think Surrealism influenced him more in
his prose than in his verse. In the verse the problem of
the poet was rather expression, whereas in the prose he
has deliberately sought unusual subject-matter and the
problem is a creation of supernatural atmosphere—the
same type of problem as confronts the writers of thriller-
novels. I mean that the Surrealist element is a minor
one in the poems, but a major one in the prose.

The second number of 'Contemporary Poetry and
Prose' coincided with the Surrealist Exhibition, and was
a special Surrealist number containing work by all the
leading Surrealists, mostly translated by the younger
poets. Roger Roughton was intending sooner or later
to produce an immense Surrealist anthology, and in
successive numbers printed a great deal of translated
work by Breton, Eluard, Péret, Lautréamont, Tzara,
Picasso and many others, as well as a good selection of
advanced writing from America, Russia, Spain and other
countries. His review, whatever its faults, was perhaps
the most international review produced in the 'thirties,
with the exception of 'Transition', which also played an
important part in the dissemination of Surrealism.

David Gascoyne is, I think, the only English writer
who integrally accepted Surrealism and abandoned himself to its tender mercies. Apart from his book and
numerous translations, he published in 'Contemporary
Poetry and Prose' several parts of his long poem 'The
Symptomatic World', which is a very interesting, if
obscure, production. The greatest objection that can be
raised against his Surrealist poems is that they sometimes

appear forced—as though they were concocted rather than spontaneously written—but 'The Symptomatic World' as a whole seems very genuine and has not this fault. Although I do not profess to 'understand' it, I can feel the emotional truth of this poem in lines like

> And the seat of the soul is the mouth of the stone
> Which is why the earth's veins are so stopped up with sand
> And the sea is so full of green flame
> For the earth is a kiss on the mouth of the sky
> And the sky is a fan in the hand of the sun.

One has the impression that Gascoyne has been trying to 'live down' his Surrealist period. It is true that he started printing at an unusually early age, but those early poems are nothing to be ashamed of. In spite of occasional triviality they all showed a great personal integrity, and above all a fine sense of rhythm which no amount of Surrealism could dispel. Readers might look at some of the poems which later appeared in 'New Verse', some very good poems in 'Poetry' (London), and especially those four poems which he intercalated among his translations from Hölderlin. The poem 'Tenebrae', for instance, shows a capacity for delicate and sensitive writing:

> The granite organ in the crypt
> Resounds with rising thunder through the blood
> With daylight song, unearthly song that floods
> The brain with bursting suns:
> Yet it is night
> It is the endless night, whose every star
> Is in the spirit like the snow of dawn,
> Whose meteors are the brilliance of summer,
> And whose wind and rain
> Are all the halcyon freshness of the valley rivers,
> Where the swans,
> White, white in the light of dream,
> Shall dip their heads.

There is evidence that the recent influence of Jean-Jouve on Gascoyne has been good, and that the best of his talent is now developing.

It was amusing at the same time to see 'New Verse' coquetting with Surrealism, in some interesting anonymous objections, some rather pontifical statements by Hugh Sykes Davies, and some Surrealist prose-poems by a cobbler. It is yet one more tribute to the breadth of 'New Verse' that many of the young poets who now indulged in Surrealism were also connected with that periodical. There was Bernard Gutteridge, who in Number 4 of 'Contemporary Poetry and Prose' printed an astonishing poem beginning 'She, making a leopard of the po'—a type of poem which it is hard to attribute to either Surrealism or 'New Verse' methods of observation. There was A. J. M. Smith, who had rather a silly poem in Number 7 :

> Meanwhile Mr Baldwin
> Managed to make himself heard.
> He looked sad
> But with characteristic aplomb said
> Keep calm there is no cause for alarm . . .
> Two soldiers' crutches had sexual intercourse
> On the spot with a little bit of fluff
> From a lint bandage in the firing chamber
> Of a 12-inch gun. . . .

Not quite so silly as it looks, perhaps, since it has been demonstrated more than once that Surrealism provides a very effective weapon of unrestricted satire. Or there was Humphrey Jennings, who at the Surrealist Exhibition in London presented a photograph of Lord Kitchener, or some such person, with the sub-title 'The Minotaur'. He printed many amusing prose pieces, purporting to come from a book on Lord Byron, as well as numerous prose-poems made by extracting bits from newspapers and sticking them together. One of his 'Reports' is a good instance of Surrealist humour, with that basis of reality which prevents it from being nonsense:

> When the horse is impassioned with love, desire, or appetite, he shows his teeth, twinkles his coloured eyes, and seems to laugh.
> He shows them also when he is angry and would bite; and volumes of smoke come from his ears.
> He sometimes puts out his tongue to lick. His mouth consists of the two rays of the eternal twins, cool as a sea breeze.

Or there was Roy Fuller, whose dragon and crime poems showed how easy it is to link up the 'poetic unreason' of the Graves school with Surrealism. The poems of George Barker which appeared in the same review are of the same category as Dylan Thomas's; they touch Surrealism superficially.

Roger Roughton was engaged on a long, semi-Surrealist novel called 'The Largest Imaginary Ball-room in the World'. I do not know if it was ever finished: it was an extraordinary production which revealed a great deal of imagination and a capacity for minute reporting of reality. His poems were rather cerebral and lacked any personal sense of rhythm. At the same time, I was busy translating the 'Songs of Maldoror' of Lautréamont, but although I followed Surrealism enthusiastically, I was as far as these other poets from being a real Surrealist. I considered it only as a means to an end, and not as an end to itself. I still think it is possible, and perhaps a good thing, for a poet to write automatically for his own purposes, as a way of getting his mind to work freely and spontaneously. After that, however, the artist in him must do a certain amount of selecting and editing. My only really Surrealist poem, which I left as it occurred to me (written in five minutes), was called 'Billet-Doux':

Looking through the blue key-hole of your eye
Into your lawn, the tall tree walks towards me
Hurls me fat fruits, eats me with caterpillars.
I am devoured by ants, by hedgehogs, by the owl's nostalgia,
For love is so hard, so very hard, to forgive.
Your spirit crawls to me across the grass,
Takes me with tentacles and buries me alive
Inside your heart: I write with your best blood.

Other poems, such as 'The Merry Window', 'Ode in
Honour', were also Surrealist, but had been slightly
vetted. The poem 'Defence of Gothic', which looked
very Surrealist, was actually suggested by an extremely
prosy essay in the 'Nouvelle Revue Française' ('Limites,
non frontières du Surrealisme') by André Breton, in
which he spoke in praise of Gothic castles and cathedrals.

One of the few English Surrealist books I know of, produced at that time, was Hugh Sykes Davies's prose-poem,
'Petron'. This work was very obviously inspired by
Lautréamont's 'Maldoror', and a Surrealist objection
against it would be that it was obviously censored. But it
contained some excellent parts, such as the scene in the
forest where the trees uproot themselves and march in
Petron's wake. The book as a whole, though, seems to
me to belong more to our own Romantic tradition of
'fine-writing' than to the new Surrealist movement:

> He passes on along the darkening canyon, its sides veined
> with curious ores which, catching the failing light, cast lurid
> and unnatural gleams across the gloom. Boulders beset his
> solitary path, and fallen crags which, worn to outlandish
> shapes, seem to be rising from a sleep. Along the cliffs
> the dubious wind sets up a dismal howl that almost drowns
> the advancing thunder. The coppery sun sinks in a swirl-
> ing mist, and in his bloody light we catch our last glimpse
> of Petron, now climbing ledge to ledge the dizzy wall,
> groping for footholds in the living rock. The clouds sweep
> down into the abyss, and he is lost to our sight.

Surrealism has been rapidly transformed into something

constructive in our modern English poetry, and at no time has it fully dominated writers as it did in France. Perhaps the best neo-Surrealist work in English has been in prose: the fine prose-poems of George Barker, Davies's 'Petron', and some parts of that excellent first novel, Ruthven Todd's 'Over the Mountain'.

June 1941.

THE APOCALYPSE

Nicholas Moore, Henry Treece, J. F. Hendry, G. S. Fraser, etc.

THERE are signs that the great movement of liberation begun by Surrealism, or privately achieved by such poets as George Barker and Dylan Thomas, is now being continued and systematized by some of the younger writers, who are trying to give it a more positive direction. These younger writers have formed into a group known as 'The Apocalypse'. They have already published two collective books, 'The New Apocalypse' (Fortune Press, 1939) and 'The White Horseman' (Routledge, 1941), as well as being particularly active for three years in America, where they have published most of their work and founded a group called 'The International Workshop', which they later left in almost entirely American hands.

The main aims of the movement have been fairly completely expressed by the main leaders, Henry Treece, G. S. Fraser and J. F. Hendry. After a meeting in 1938 they decided on the following points:

(1) That Man was in need of greater freedom, economic no less than aesthetic, from machines and mechanistic thinking.

(2) That no existent political system, Left or Right; no artistic ideology, Surrealism or the political school of Auden, was able to provide this freedom.

(3) That the Machine Age had exerted too strong an influence on art, and had prevented the individual development of Man.

(4) That Myth, as a personal means of reintegrating the personality, had been neglected and despised.

I do not think that any poet fully alive to the conditions of our time would disagree with these points, with the possible exception of their political implications, which might leave the writer to be crushed more than ever between the Left and Right, which, however imperfectly, represent a real division between men's aspirations and view of the world. In 1940 the group tried to clarify this aspect of their beliefs, saying they leaned towards 'A special form of Anarchism . . . and which implies collective ownership of small local groups, working as far as possible under conditions conducive to individual action'. This is a dream of many free-thinking men of our time, but, apart from setting up colonies as similar Utopists like Cabet did a hundred years ago, or apart from beginning some vast revolution, there seems little likelihood of this being achieved. The principle is there, however, and it is one which shows that some of the teachings of D. H. Lawrence are still very much alive today, emerging into the doctrine of the new priest of Anarchism, Mr Herbert Read.

But we are not for the moment concerned with the political side of this programme: what is more important is whether it foreshadows some renaissance in poetry and the other arts. In Great Britain our writers, unlike those of the Continent, are not usually given to collective programmes, and that is why, ever since the Symbolist movement, the initiative has lain with the writers of the Continent. That these writers are young should make no difference: their collective action is significant. And they, alas, will be old all too soon. But in the meantime it is in their hands that the destiny of our poetry might be shaped after the war.

The Apocalyptic movement is to mean liberation from a purely objective world, a reaction against the objective reporting of the 'thirties, against mass-observation and the parochial conception of 'observing' which was evolved by the followers of Auden and Grigson. Its literary ancestors are said to be Revelations, Shakespeare, Webster, Blake, Donne, Hopkins and Kafka. . . .

I cannot say what Donne really has to do with it. Here is a prejudice unquestionably taken up from the Eliot generation. Donne, who under his clerical dress cleaned up a few of the scattered ends of the Renaissance, but who, far from being a liberator, reflects in his tortuous and painful style an ingrown nature; whose acceptance of the authority of Church and State suggests that today on a political plane he might have been a Fascist Laureate, and whose intellectual honesty was brought into question as soon as he allowed himself, or pretended, to quake at the thought of Hell. Nor has Hopkins any real affinity with the Apocalypse or with any such movement. Hopkins, also far from being a liberator, was a great but *thwarted* sensualist, a stuffed and stifled D. H. Lawrence of Jesuitry and Victorianism. He sneakingly hated yet sympathized with the new Socialist movement, and repressed all his truest human feelings at the command of his implacable 'superiors'. He is a man who disguised himself as a priest, and who was obliged to disguise his primitive and sensual reactions to the world under a hollow vocabulary of worship. Technically, as a metrician and stylist, he was a liberator, and here his attraction for the new movement can be understood, but the inclusion of his name so close to those of Blake and Webster shows a radical misunderstanding of his real achievement.

From the rather frightening but interesting essay by J. F. Hendry, 'Writers of the Apocalypse', emerge especially the emphasis on the word 'Organic' and much praise for Dylan Thomas and Kafka. Apocalyptic writing is 'Concerned with the study of living, the collapse of social forms and the emergence of new and more organic ones'. Here I am in complete agreement: we are in great need of a revolution against the arbitrary academic tradition of poetic form, which has little conception of the nature of poetry and replaces such a conception by the counting of stresses and syllables and a stuffy notion of decorum. Then there is a great insistence on myth, man as myth, which is one of the most original ideas of this school: Hendry speaks of 'The symbolic or prophetic aspect of myth, (which) consists in the projection of the self which it actually involves in everyday life'. This mythological element, of course, was already present in Surrealism, which, with its materialist basis, tried to mythologize the relationship of man to nature. G. S. Fraser quite rightly admits that the Apocalypse is, as it were, a 'dialectical development of Surrealism, embodying all that is positive in Surrealism'.

Apocalypse is, then, a de-mechanizing, or a dematerializing, of Surrealism. Above all, the individual is to be liberated from that purely clinical interest in the workings of the mind which the Surrealists were almost promoting into a new religion. The Apocalyptic writers intend to use this very deliberately and not be slaves to it, and, according to Hendry, they will exalt the choice and control of the artist. Hendry writes: 'Artists more responsible than the Surrealists find that art is not merely the juxtaposition of images not commonly juxtaposed, but the recognition, the communication of organic experience, experience with personal shape, experience which (however wild and startling in content) is a formal whole.' This insistence on the experience of art as 'formal whole' is the only guarantee of sanity offered by the Apocalyptic writers. Apart from that, the movement may be summed up as a drive for individual expression and integrity, expressed in the terms: 'To have social values, poetry does not need to show *immediate* political relevance. . . . The struggle to be classic, social, relevant and so on is unnecessary; because if a poet describes honestly his private perspective on the world, his private universe, human minds are sufficiently analogous to each other for that private universe to become (ultimately but certainly not immediatcly) a generally accessible human property.' It is certainly true that a poet's first task must be to understand and express himself. But in spite of so many safeguards as the 'sufficiently', 'ultimately', etc., in the above passage, the only standards by which the Apocalyptics can be judged are those which they have laid down in the present. For the poet's self-understanding is necessary, but is at first his own business. His self-expression more immediately concerns us: we can legitimately ask: Has he expressed himself in terms which, since he is using our common language, mean anything to us, and, secondly, if this is his experience, has it any value for us? That is to say, a school of poets cannot be judged merely by whether the poets have achieved what they intended to do: they must also be judged by the actual quality of the pudding they have produced.

It is in this respect that, so far, much of the Apocalyptic work is rather disappointing. In prose, their first anthology contained a first-rate essay on Picasso by H. Melville and an excellent story about a political concentration-camp by J. F. Hendry, but some quite incomprehensible prose by Dorian Cooke, who elsewhere shows himself a possible but not an impressive poet. I can make nothing of the poems of Norman McCaig, whose only modification of the surrealist-catalogue poem is that he divides it up into stanzas of equal length. Philip O'Connor is an ingenious Left humorist, whose poems are always attractive but never very profound. One does not need to belong to such a movement to write:

> The baby should have oranges, which run through him
>   nourishingly
> He would then make more noise,
> We would wash him, he would shine like silver spoons.

No, the only poets of importance in the movement are Dylan Thomas, Henry Treece and Nicholas Moore (in that order), followed by Fraser, Hendry and Tom Scott. Hendry's ability is rather limited to giving a generalized expression of an emotion, and when, for instance, the emotion is as large a one as that produced by the Spanish war, there is obviously little difficulty in presenting it immediately, as he does in his 'Picasso—for Guernica', in lines like

> Splint for the shriven sin I foster mantrump out
> Of festered history; sprout pointed fingers
> Where an afterbirth is dung and rubble-teat.
> I am the eyeball blown world! Axis of anger!

Too much of this is verbal, a conjuring-trick, and such a poem fades into its right place when confronted with a really created study of fear such as Picasso's painting 'Guernica'. Since that poem, Hendry has developed considerably, and though he writes sometimes gushingly ('Miraculous dissolution of bombast and lust in an ele-mental Marlborough') he can also write with a great restraint and purity:

> Though the leaves crowd, in galaxies of shaken stars,
> Driving towards my window like a clipper-ship,
> I turn away. In our society
> Men demand surfeit of food, a place to sleep.
> We cannot learn from leaves to live on air.

> Though flowers are without desire, and all fruit falls soon
>   after
> Fellowed, we live fearfully, hoard ourselves in lovers.

HENRY TREECE

Our societies are not trees,
Nor have we joy like these tempestuous shivering leaves, or
Their collaboration of bells in untold laughter.

Now this looks much purer than it really is. This poem is an allegorical presentation of the Anarchist conception of an organic society. Hendry points to the trees and flowers and sees in their lives an example of organic pattern which is not followed in human societies. A simple theme, which could have been thoroughly worked out and lost none of the beauty of its development in being more logical. For do men demand a 'surfeit' of food? Leaves do not 'live on air', they live on food drawn, like man's, from the soil. Research in botany is far from showing that flowers are 'without desire', unless Hendry means 'all their desires are satisfied', which is again questionable. Fruits are never 'fellowed'. The rest about the 'joy' of leaves is pure superstition. Now all these inaccuracies would be quite admissible in a lyrical poem about nature, in which the poet was trying to express the emotions aroused in him. The pathetic fallacy is a purely legitimate way of interpreting nature. But in a poem like this, where the poet is actually confronting nature and society and comparing them, these poetic falsehoods are less admissible. And in any case it will be noticed that Hendry is falling into that strangest of all misconceptions of our Romantic poets, the idea of man as something distinct from nature. It is true that he desires the opposite, but in effect he insists on man's differences from nature. This poem should be one instance of how individualist logic can fail in its application to details, even when a poet has, in his private life, a sensible and homogeneous outlook in life.

This does not alter the fact that Hendry's poems in 'The White Horseman' show him to be a poet worth watching. His war poems, 'Sonnet in Wartime', 'Mid-

F

night Air Raid' and 'A Winter of War', while being written partly in the overtones usually associated with war poems, show a gravity and power of direct statement as well as a maturity of vision. Almost the only sign of his membership of the Apocalyptic group is his reliance upon Biblical symbolism, which he has in common with many of the young admirers of Dylan Thomas. He can write with an admirable precision which shows that the Apocalypse does not stand merely for wild writing. The poem 'A Winter of War' is in fact an ingenious series of parallels between the war and the season, and it contains vignettes which occasionally remind one of the landscapes of the baroque minor French poets of the early seventeenth century, such as Théophile and St-Amant:

> All foliage, of tree or bough,
> Yields to the peering hunter
> Whose tracks, invisible as winter,
> Bulge white and huge as snow.

So long as Hendry can show such a sense of balance— which is rivalled in the group only by the marmorean style of Vernon Watkins, who, however, has only slight affinities with the others—there is hope that the movement will attract other poets and admirers who are drawn more by such work as this than by the theory of any school.

G. S. Fraser writes with ease, charm and grace. He has achieved fluency, but he can do nothing in verse that cannot be done better by his friend Nicholas Moore, who also has a great deal more variety. Fraser has developed young, and though his poems are youthful they have the ease which is that of promise and not merely of habit. But I think he is still too much in the wake of the Byronic Auden:

> All this is egoism, as I know.
> Let me be sand and sensible and flat.

> Perhaps the healthy impulse will persist,
> Although it interrupts the lyric flow.
> All I have written might boil down to that—
> Well, nobody can love an egoist!

Undistinguished writing, which is by no means on a level with Fraser's excellent and persuasive prose.

Of the remaining poets there is one, Tom Scott, who is little known, but who shows great promise. He used to be a stone-mason, and his poetry has a naïve quality unspoilt by the literary background which intrudes into too much poetry today. His writing seems to come straight from his inner consciousness, and if his themes are limited, his rhythms are instinctive and his imagery fresh, but the simplicity of the poems is deceptive, for a great deal of suffering and conflict is to be felt beneath it:

> I found him drowned on the rock that night
> And the wind high; moonlight it was
> And the hungry sucking of the sea
> At my feet and his clammy head in my breasts
> That were bare as the rock and the sea and the sand.

We are likely to gain a new lyric poet if he can retain the purity of vision and spontaneity of such lines as:

> Listening to the harp of stone that grants
> No rest for this forsaken hill and no return
> No release shall be my lot and never urn
> Of angel spill to bless my plants;

or:

> And since my silence breaks at last
> The topaz bridles of hair rein the seven seas.

Dylan Thomas has also some connection with this movement, especially as a sort of mascot or Apocalyptic Hero. His peculiar talents really do fit very well into the Apocalyptic framework of anarchism, myth, personal discovery. Many of the things I have said in another essay about Dylan Thomas apply to Treece. That is not to say that Treece is a second edition of Dylan Thomas. It is true that he has written a book about Thomas, and that some of his early poems were very like Thomas's. They have a very common background, both being Welshmen, admirers of Hopkins and Joyce, readers of the Bible and ballads, and having the Welsh gift of the gab. But although Treece's twenty-five sonnets in his 'Towards a Personal Armageddon' are similar in atmosphere and climate to Thomas's, and similar in texture, it is evident on a closer reading that Treece has adapted Thomas's discoveries to different ends. Treece's early poems were over-rich, but with a richness which is that of a young poet conscious of his own power. Less disciplined than Thomas, his syntax was none the less easier, his vocabulary less disturbing and his rhythms more fluid :

> Yet song was there, growing through the lids,
> Gradual, child-footed, wanting but the grave
> To snap the leash and cast it into light.
> Now cries the blood and the plucked bone cries,
> And only the heart still as nerveless hands
> Scatter the perfect years, the perfect years.

If a poet is not rich when he is young, he will be for ever poor. And this atmosphere of poetry, which creates itself so rapidly in the writing of Treece as in Thomas, is something peculiar to the Welsh and Irish poets, a gift which cannot be acquired save by long acquaintance with a restricted culture. Now Treece is obviously refining the personal mythology which was the whole subject of his 'Armageddon' poems, and which is extremely hard to decipher. In his later poems he is coming nearer to folklore, and no doubt discovering that a personal mythology is only strengthened when it is brought to the level of the popular imagination. He has deliberately turned to the legend and fairy-tale of the past, and seems to be engaged in interpreting the present world in terms of them. His

later poems are full of princes, magicians, strange old men
and suffering girls. And this is, perhaps, the secret of the
Celtic imagination, this ability to see people as symbols:

> I spilled the oil of my wonder, spilled my tears,
> Through the clouds of dismay: I watched them go,
> Trailing like phantoms across the heath,
> Where the three old men knelt, sad in prayer.

As soon as he writes '*the* clouds' instead of 'clouds', and
'*the* three old men' instead of 'three old men', these
things seem to assume a deeper significance. Or again:

> The song that the old woman sings in the lane
> Is the song of the girl with the golden hair,
> Of the gaunt old man who danced in the rain,
> And the soldiers who ran from his eyes in fear.

Or consider this piece of fine writing from 'Saint Agnes':

> Mary she moves, with more than Mary-grace,
> Among the grey, unleavened progeny of stone,
> Past the slow vastness of the sodden byre.
> The ancient word that festers in her breast
> Wails like a wasp and stirs her blood to song. . . .

His recent poems as a whole show, side by side with this
revival of mediaeval legend and atmosphere, a deepening
religious sense which might ultimately lead him far away
from his first conception of personal myth. But however
he develops, allegiance to a movement can neither help
nor hinder him: the essential thing is there, that purity
and innocence which breathes from some of his poems in
his sequence 'The Ballad of the Prince', such as:

> Brief months ago I loved a merry girl,
> Whose fingers wove with mine a merry game.
> While our flocks mingled, mingled was our tale
> Of faith, and fullness and the fire-lit home.
> Long days were dwarfed, quicksilvered by our glee,
> The swallow taught our love the way to dance,
> We learned from lambing-time the way to pray. . . .

Nicholas Moore also contributes some positive writing to the Apocalypse. In his book 'A Wish in Season' at least half the poems are well conceived and well made. Many of those which fail, do so because they are unpleasantly exhibitionist: 'I still remember, darling, the warmth of your legs'. Some poems, like 'Poem for Billie Holiday', are directly trivial. Some of the poems about his childhood have that precocious nastiness of Rimbaud's early poems, especially 'The Bird with Several Faces', which is perversely beautiful, and 'Prayer to Nobody', which is impoverished neo-Dylan Thomas.

But there is something positive in Moore's book. The war, for instance, which is sometimes a strenuous test for poets, produces some of his deepest feeling and his best work:

> O refugee and visiting stranger, have mercy,
> Look with a cold eye on our crooked landscape, and wish for
> Peace that will break with new fire, as the people
>   Free this dear country.   ('Poem for This Wartime')

It is certainly a good thing that a young poet should exercise his talent on everyday things and events, and Moore for one has greatly widened his interests and scope in the course of the war. His two sonnets, 'Memorial Sonnet' and 'Across the Atlantic', show a hitherto undeveloped power of concentration, and a fine sustained effort worthy of a mature poet:

> O no, death is not ample, nor how bravely
> He lived in a sinking ship sufficient reason,
> Who was so kind in life. For him this simple
> Political moment held a new town like heaven
> To be built by his kindly eyes, but his instructions
> Failed, not for the future now, but for the present.
>   ('Memorial Sonnet')

Moore is also very successful in some personal poems,

in 'Epistle to E. B. C.' and the poem for George Barker, and especially in one or two political poems. One of these latter, 'Charley didn't have a new master', is a good combination of wit and feeling, while 'The Star' is a love poem on a grand scale. Moore's great characteristic, although he appears to suppress it, is a very precious quality of gentleness, as seen in 'Poem':

> You look like history. All the bright caravans
> That ended in no more than a madman's whisper,
> The cavalcade of honour that led to death,
> Is history you have loved and suffered beneath. . . .
>
> You look like fable, myth, and the fairy tale,
> But you are real as the boy was in the stable.
> What agony is to suffer will still be true,
> Though the future open out like a flower in you.

This lyric is perhaps the best he has written, and if Moore can continue being free within this self-imposed discipline which is shaping his best poems, and diminish the Auden and Thomas influence, he has a future as a poet.

Moore's poems in his second book, 'The Island and the Cattle', and in 'The White Horseman', show that he is developing surely as a lyric poet, and class him as one of the purest writers among the younger generation. He still has serious lapses of taste—half the poems in 'The Island and the Cattle', for instance, have little claim to the reader's attention—but this is fully outweighed by his positive qualities. He writes as spontaneously as Paul Eluard, and with the same directness about politics as about love:

> Do I make my disasters clear? The wind from Mexico
> Blows up its rumours and I let it go,
> Or does it chase a white sun from the heavens?
> . . . The people lift their hands and wait the end.
> O Democracy, where is your sunny tree?

And he can combine humour with tenderness in a way which is characteristic of the best English folk-songs:

> The wind is a girl's heart,
> The wind is an apple in the spring,
> The wind is an horseshoe swinging on a gate.
>
> I offered her an orchard of trees hung with nails,
> I offered her a basket of deer,
> She took only the eye from my lap.
>
> But there's deer in the orchard,
> My apples are yours for the picking.
> Dear, I only want the horseshoe and the honest truth.

Moore is writing spontaneously, constantly running the risk of looking foolish—and occasionally being so—and writing perhaps a little too much. It cannot be too often stressed that spontaneity does not mean an uninterrupted flow of production. The poet's life should be an ardent preparation for spontaneity: he should all the time be training himself in his art and in the art of living, so that when the time comes for him to speak, his words will readily assume the shape of his thoughts and feelings. But the constant flow can mean the dissipation of energy into occasional good lines wrapped in the dull brown paper of mediocrity. I do not suggest that Moore is at any times mediocre, for his delicacy and sense of humour preserve him from that, but it is certain that he is rich enough to prune his work a little and keep it to the level of his best achievements. And the same can be said of the Apocalyptic poets as a whole: having explored their capacities, it is now their task to achieve a synthesis.

December 1941.

OBSERVATIONS ON POETRY AND WAR

I

In writing on this subject, around which there is bound to be great controversy before the war is over, there is little the critic can do save to set out his own opinions and await contradiction. In this battle criticism will be keenest when directed by the 'War Poets' of 1914-1918 against the poets of the present generation, who have already been accused in the newspapers of not rising to the occasion. It will be bitterest when voiced by the young poets, whose many gestures since the war began have been ignored or misunderstood; it will be most cynical, perhaps, from those who, slightly older but not yet middle-aged, played Cassandra for ten years before this war broke out, and who have withdrawn hurriedly from the arena. And most of the battle will be futile until some effort is made at defining the poet's rôle in war-time, which is about as difficult in appearance, but less so in reality, as defining what poets ought to do in peace.

There are at least two kinds of 'war poetry': a specialized type which is 'about' the war, uncrowned-Poet-Laureate poetry such as every war evokes, and in which poets proceed to lay down the law. Then there is poetry of the 'Business as usual' type which professes to ignore the war, and which is 'war poetry' only—and none the less—because a war is happening while it is being written. Then there are at least, superficially, two kinds of 'War Poets': those who are in uniform, and those who are not. People are curiously respectful of the difference which a uniform makes to a poet—to such an extent that one of them signs himself publicly as 'Gunner', as

though such a title gave him more merit than his legitimate and well-earned one of 'Poet'. It is to be hoped
that a poet can still be a poet these days in spite of being
a Gunner or an Auxiliary Fireman. And the uniformed
and civilian 'War Poets' also have their kinds, to an
extent which seriously affects their poetry and their
public. There are those who are, or affect to be, indifferent to the war, those who acclaim it in some respects,
and those who are its violent opponents. . . . It should be
at once evident that the problem cannot be approached
on such a muddled basis, for that is what has been happening for some time among some very enlightened
people. We must, then, attempt to reduce the problem
by reaching some of the general principles lying behind it.

War or no war, poetry is not a thing of the moment,
that is to say, writing with nothing more than its immediate topical appeal. Poetry must be built to last. There
is all the difference between much war verse and poetry
as there is between a tent and a house. This does not
mean that good integral war poetry cannot be written.
We have behind us the admirable 'Les Tragiques' of
D'Aubigné on the French religious wars of the Reforma-
tion; we have the great Classical Epics, the Northern
Ballads, the Eddas and Sagas, to remind us that poetry
can spring as well from the heroisms and tortures of war
as from the delights and disappointments of peace. On
this basis I am tempted to lay down what seem to me
almost axiomatic principles affecting poetry and war.

A good war poem must also be a good peace poem.

In order to write such a poem, in war or peace, a poet
must be a poet, must have, that is to say, a strength and
delicacy of feeling somewhat above the average, and a
background of personal thought and experience which he
has learnt technically to express and psychologically to
disclose without fear. He must know his language as

well as he knows what is happening in and around him.

As for having the necessary 'experience' of war, it is impossible, in this war especially, to lay down any inclusive definition of 'war experience'. To my mind, the best poems springing from war are not necessarily written by those young poets who have handled guns, sat in cockpits or slept in barracks. This is especially the case at the present time, when the civilians of every country are literally military objectives, and when there is little distinction between soldier and civilian save that the former is better armed, better organized and better protected for the conditions in which he has to live and die, though it is also agreed that the civilian is better paid.

In this connection it will be observed that some of the best 'war poems' of the Great War were written by Americans. We shall have to seek far in order to find anything deeper on the subject than Ezra Pound's 'Mauberly' and Eliot's 'The Waste Land', the one expressing with such concentrated feeling the bitter disappointment of a civilized man, and the second giving a synthesis of the post-war spiritual depression. There was one other really great poem, greater perhaps than either of the above, and that was Paul Valéry's 'La Jeune Parque', which, written in the war, so triumphantly asserted the life-principle at a time when living, so precarious and so bound with pain as it then was, had been rendered, as it always is in war, more precious than his generation had ever dreamed. If in war-time we seek persuasion of the beauty of natural existence, we can do no better than to turn to such a poem.

What happens only too frequently to those who too directly participate in warfare, in destruction and bloodshed, is that their poetry tends to overflow the emotional bounds of words and become hysterical. The bitter

laments of Wilfred Owen and the violent caustic rage of
Siegfried Sassoon in the last war seem to me to fall into
this fault just as much as the frantically nostalgic poems
of Apollinaire's unforgettable 'Calligrammes', in spite of
an occasional refreshing sweetness. As for the poetry
which springs from hatred, I address my readers to Paul
Fort's lamentable poem, written on the destruction of
Rheims Cathedral—the cathedral of his home town—
addressed to the 'Monstrous General Von Plattenburg',
on whom he proceeded to spit his contempt, as upon
everything German. We can take warning from the fact
that Paul Fort, during the last war, was perhaps the most
popular poet in France, and as soon as it was over, the
most speedily neglected. The same fate attends, I believe,
the virulent hate-poems of Lord Vansittart which besmirch
the 'Sunday Times' on Sabbath mornings. Partisanship
is of little avail, and is a poor friend of poetry, when it
does not co-exist with some broader and more ennobling
human quality. Lord Vansittart's poems are certainly of
some merit as propaganda, but I think it can be said
they are too one-sided, whereas the poet, instead of having
a one-track mind, should be, above all men, capable of
seeing both sides of any question with equal clarity and
sympathy. That is what Baudelaire meant when he said
he could understand a man deserting one side to serve
another: he meant that the poet's curiosity is such that
he cannot admit that white and black necessarily contra-
dict each other. However good they might be as propaganda, these poems of Lord Vansittart's are based on
an extreme of hatred, in vivid contrast to the Chris-
tian sentiments which in the same breath he professes
to hold. To assume that the Germans are and always
have been 'Butcher-birds' is the surest way of misunderstanding the finer points of this war, or of missing them
entirely. The great tragedy of our times, and of our

destiny, is not merely that 'butcher-birds' in the shape of Germans, Italians, Hungarians, Roumanians and Bulgarians are destroying civilization, but that civilized peoples are destroying each other, civilization is destroying itself. Let us admit for a moment that the Germans might be human (or were until 1939, 1933, 1914 or 1870), and that they might be to a high degree civilized, intelligent and feeling; then the horror of the situation becomes one which calls for tears, prayer and resolution rather than for hysterical and indiscriminating rage.

The best war poems (as indicated by Eliot and Valéry) may have no ostensible bearing on war, and yet gain significance in relation to such events.

Moreover, the best war poems are not necessarily written *during* a war. We can remember the sudden rush of 'war novels' and war films in the 'twenties. Many of those novels had been written years before and hidden away for future reference, but a greater number were written after the experience of war had been thoroughly assimilated. War must be digested and seen in perspective before any sustained work can be produced to serve as its monument. The greatest novel produced in France—perhaps in the world—was Marcel Proust's catacomb of introspection, 'A La Recherche du Temps Perdu'. And on the other hand, Tristan Tzara's book 'L'Homme Approximatif', the longest and most terrifying war poem I have read, was not written and published until the late 'twenties. Victor Hugo's fine series of poems on the Napoleonic Legend were written years after the event ('Waterloo', if I remember rightly, was not written until 1852), by a poet who had merely passed a part of his childhood in the Napoleonic era, and in whom had been ingrained a deep hatred and contempt for his later hero. It is a curious fact that in France little or nothing of any value, in verse, was written about the Napoleonic Wars while they lasted, and that the French Revolution itself produced its great singers not in France but in Britain. If the present war has witnessed the writing of two poems of first rank, they are Eliot's 'East Coker' and 'The Dry Salvages', which, far from being meditations on the ruins of London or the fate of Europe, are variations on the problems of time and eternity in their relation to human life, a subject obviously of less topical interest but of perennial value and importance.

This is, perhaps, the most important point. The best war poetry is necessarily written not by those who *see* war, but by those who *feel* it most intensely. That is why being a soldier, though it will not necessarily harm a poet, will not necessarily help him. Provided he has not lost all capacity for feeling, a poet's migration to America—as in the case of Barker and Auden—does not preclude his writing a good poem arising from the tragedy of Europe. Auden's 'Letter in Wartime' was a near miss, and one which, while for the moment it might not meet our expectations, we shall perhaps more fully appreciate at a later date when all its implications are more fully realized. If the premiss from which we start here is true, that poetry is the privilege of those who feel, then good poetry, whether it concern the war or not, can at the present time be written alike by German and Briton, American and Italian; by pacifist and militarist, by Nazi and democrat, by internationalist as well as by patriot. Each of these will feel in his own life some vital element of the truth of the situation and its relation to human destiny: each will be attracted to singing the praise of the great human emotions, good and bad, which are aroused by war: courage, hatred, nostalgia, contempt, love for man, woman and child, or for a vast army of conflicting ideals. But to do this at all well, the heart will need to be pure and the mind clear, and what is happening at the present time among the English poets is that too few of them are so blessed.

II

Because of their age, many of the younger poets are serving in the Forces, some eager, some reluctant, others indifferent. Faced with unaccustomed discipline, discomforts and petty annoyances, the poetic Private finds ample time for his ardour to cool, whether on the barrack square or in the boundless futility of some African desert. He is thus almost better placed than the average civilian to realize how deeply and subtly war spreads into the roots of one's being, alternately stimulating and corroding the most delicate fibres of the soul. He will often think of the past, longing for it, but sometimes regretting that 'sad, waste time', and reproaching himself for many an action or word loosed in the heat of the moment. He might be trying, as he eats a stubborn meal, or as he creeps into his shoddy, chafing blankets, to reconcile his former pacifism with his conscript's uniform, or his eagerness for the war to be won with his reluctance to bear its ordeals. In pubs, cinemas and canteens he ponders heavily, fitfully, over the shape of post-war society; as he writes letters home, or to his creditors, he wonders how either of them, and himself, will ever make ends meet; he wonders whether he will find a job after the war, and, if he has the misfortune to be a specialist, how long it will take him to re-equip his mind or his hands for tasks which once he performed with ease. As regards poetry, once his pastime or his daily labour and delight, he finds the urge to write less frequently upon him, because he lacks the energy, the solitude or the company he had with deliberation cultivated, the landscapes, the streets, the buildings and the music he once cherished. Worse still, when he does feel like writing, he discovers that sergeants and parades wait for no poet: work accumulates unfinished in his mind, and by the time he finds occasion to sit down and take up the pen, his thoughts wander and he finds nothing to record.

But because there is a war, that does not mean that life does not continue, in its essentials, much as before. People must eat, drink, sleep and love; trees, birds and flowers weave their mysterious lives, the sun still peers through mosaics of cloud, there are still children smiling and young girls growing to womanhood, and the moon still casts her gown on soldier and civilian alike. It is a mistake, then, for any poet in uniform to forget these marvels which will outlast his present trials, and it is a mistake for readers of poetry to look anxiously for innumerable poems about Bren guns, tanks, or the national morale. Certainly, some good things of this kind have been written. As I march on parade I sometimes think of Gavin Ewart's 'The Bofors A.A. Gun', but though I have a pleasant opinion of Gavin Ewart, and though I think it is still possible to write well about such things—for it is possible to write well about anything, and Marinettism is not yet dead—that is not the type of poem I most willingly recall. What cannot be readily forgotten is that poem by Day Lewis called 'Where are the War Poets?' in which he speaks of 'defending the bad against the worse'; a consoling poem in its way, for he at least suggests the enemy is defending the worse against the bad. Then there are certain stanzas in Auden's elegies on the death of Yeats and Freud, and an incredible number of nostalgic and prophetic poems by the younger writers. Nostalgic and prophetic—these are perhaps the commonest qualities or characteristics of our war poetry at present.

Of these younger poets, Alan Rook, writing in direct contact with the war as a soldier, has most moved me, so that I know some of his work by heart. Nothing could better illustrate the mentality of 'The War Generation' of poets than his poem 'Dunkirk Pier'. Written by one whose experience proves him no shirker behind a title, an exemption or an objection, this poem, which radiates into politics and morality as such poems should do, strikes home at the unsatisfactory background of this war, and should lead our governors, if they will condescend for once to read some poetry, to think twice and prepare a programme more in harmony with the aspirations of the young than that which is the present basis of our propaganda and our home reforms. The chill horror of that disastrous episode strikes home in the opening lines, in the calm of a man awaiting death:

> Deeply across the waves of our darkness fear
> like the silent octopus feeling, groping, clear
> as a star's reflection, nervous and cold as a bird,
> tells us that pain, tells us that death is near.
>
> Why should a woman telling above her fire
> incantations of evening, thoughts that are
> older and paler than history, why should this lark
> exploring extinction and oneness of self and air
>
> Remind us that, lonely and lost as flowers in deserted
> weed-mastered gardens, each faint face averted
> from the inescapable confusion, for each of us slowly
> death on his last, most hideous journey has started.

Apart from the contrasted coldness and warmth of the first two stanzas, the simultaneous contrast of bird and lark, and the identification of the poet with that bird, and so many other intricate details which I shall not pursue

here, this is a masterpiece of controlled movement, with
that fine delay at the end of the third stanza which shows
a real understanding of eloquence.   Then there is a powerful use of the sea-image, which is identified with all the
most important elements of the whole poem.   But it is
the spirit of the poem which makes it a valuable docu-
ment, not only as an eyewitness account of a memorable
occasion, but also of the state of mind and conclusions
arising from it.   Alan Rook, in the stanzas which follow,
shows no sentimental illusion of the nature of heroism and
war: he sees war as some loathsome meal shared with
friend and enemy alike, and, replying to those Jonahs (of
whom Pétain was to be only one) who blamed the war
on the fact that people were 'too fond of life' and afraid
to learn suffering, he replies that we have learnt to suffer
all but death, and he proceeds from this to the climax
in which he seeks the broader implications of the war:

> What hope for the future?   Can we who see the tide
> ebbing along the shore, the greedy, lined
> with shadows, dare with puny words support
> a future which belongs to others?   Dare we bind
>
> Now, at this moment of sunshine above
> the crests of oncoming events, like waves which move
> remorselessly nearer, future generations
> with sacrifice?   We who taught hate, expect them to love?

This reflects a deep uneasiness for the future and our
right to determine it, it touches the fate of our children,
and above all is an admission of failure, not only in battle,
but our personal failure to direct our lives to a better end
in the past.   I cannot tell why this poem has hammered
itself into my memory: perhaps because it appeals at so
many levels and seems to penetrate into so many aspects
of our lives, or because it succeeds at once as personal
drama and public record, or because it reflects the sin-

cerest feelings of the young, or because its architectural qualities are so stimulating to the mind. Noting, for instance, that mature 'return' and extension of the sea-image in the last two stanzas, which complete and recapture fully the movement of the opening, I feel that much can be expected of a generation which is capable of such construction and poise.

So much for prophecy. The separations of war always give rise to the most characteristic of war poems, and perhaps the most permanent, the nostalgic love lyrics, which have the added attraction of appealing to doleful lovers, of whom there is no lack, long after their source of origin is forgotten. I remember chiefly a poem by Alun Lewis, and several poems of that witch of poetry, Anne Ridler, who better than any poet of our time has recaptured the spirit and habits of mind of the Metaphysicals, to such an extent that she uses their peculiar stanza-forms and groupings of phrase with no sense of incongruity. She strikes to the heart in such lines as

> I have no words to tell you what you were,
> But when you are sad, think, Heaven could give no more.

There is also a poem by Hendry beginning:

> Encompass me, my lover,
> With your eyes' wide calm;

and two other poems by the same writer, 'Midnight Air Raid' and 'Sonnet in Wartime', which are also much more than topical war poems. It is not, however, my intention to make here an anthology of my favourite war poems: all I want to show is that they exist in both large numbers and high quality. It is of great importance that the gestures and thoughts of these poets should be known and weighed, for they represent more than a cross-section of public feeling and opinion in this crisis: they represent the feeling and opinion of those who are being asked to bring that crisis to a conclusion by the sacrifice of their lives. To those who say the young are not responding to the war or writing about it, or not writing well, there is only one reply, which can be illustrated a thousand times; it is: Do you know the poem of John Waller's— an almost unknown young poet—which ends:

> Now with world breaking everywhere around us
> The *war against the past* is on, to decide now
> Whether *release* or the end. Do not escape to an island
> Or lose yourself comfortably in routine. Live
> As for love; carry the thunder of raging youth
> Hopeful to new building; live as for love.

The italics are mine. And do those people who live with their eyes shut and their ears stuffed know those lines by Nicholas Moore:

> With the coming of the morning
> More will come than our personal song,
> But it *will be a part of the people's*,
> *The revolution in the world*
> That makes a star more than a star.

Again the italics are mine. It should be evident—or, if this is not enough proof, these people might read Malla-lieu's 'Letter in Wartime', Tambimuttu's 'Out of this War' and so many others—that the young poets are thinking hard, and inclined to think a little farther than most. And at the same time it can be claimed that they are not neglecting the true task of the poet in peace and war, the preservation of the finest feelings, the highest aspirations, and the purest achievements of humanity.

III

But more important than their thoughts is the direction that poetry in their hands is taking. It is often asked whether poetry is likely to be affected in its technical aspects. It is certain that the last war did not stifle the better elements of the open-air poetry of the typical Georgians, which has reflowered in some of the younger poets. The last war, rather than creating anything new in poetry, hastened many processes which had already begun. It hastened the impressionist or symbolist method in poetry, of which Eliot, Pound and Miss Sitwell were the most outstanding exponents. It hastened also that dislocation of line and stanza which ultimately led to the peak of the free-verse period in the 'twenties, symbolized by Eliot for some, and for others by D. H. Lawrence.

In this war the movement seems in general to be rather different. We are moving towards a new Romantic movement, less irresponsible than Surrealism and Dadaism, less frantic than that represented by Lawrence, less 'literary' than that of Eliot and Pound, less restrained than the Romanticism of Herbert Read, less recondite than that of Laura Riding. Auden, with his sudden renunciation of his past, is symbolic of the radical change which is arriving both in poets and in their work. We are moving towards a more personal language on the one hand, and on the other to a profoundly sensual conception of life and poetry. So many seeds of Romanticism, planted in the past by Blake, by Byron, by Shelley, Wilde, Lawrence, Dylan Thomas, are in process of bearing fruit. Perhaps at last a great deal of theorizing will be swept aside, and in the realities of war men shall learn to write simply, sensually and passionately. Nowhere has this revolution been more clearly demonstrated than in the numbers of that struggling but valuable review, 'Poetry' (London), which have appeared during the past two years.

Apart from the theory, the undertaking did succeed in the most important sense that it drew into the pages of this review most of the young poets of any importance who are writing today. This may be only a practical problem and one which affects the circulation rather than the creation of poetry: but it is evident that 'Poetry' was a step in the right direction, and that some responsible people, inside or outside the Government, should ensure that such ventures, of inestimable value to all those who are now defending culture, should not be allowed to die for such petty reasons as paper restriction and lack of funds. Poetry is having a particularly bad time in this war: 'New Verse', 'Twentieth Century Verse', and in fact all the magazines which specialized in poetry, have been allowed to die, not at the enemy's hands, but at our own. And perhaps that explains why so many people are now crying 'Where are the War Poets?'

It is to be hoped that the young poets, who are rapidly showing themselves at once masters of the lyric and the topical commentary, will marshal their strength and work on a vaster scale than they have yet attempted. Only one poet, Tambimuttu, has yet attempted (apart from Auden) to write a long sustained poem arising from his personal experience of the war. That is not enough, and perhaps the long poem is not the surest way of reaching the people. There are other methods. First of all, the scope of these poets should be enlarged by the creation of new reviews. The newspapers should at last be coaxed or argued into opening their columns to poetry. The revival of the verse-drama begun by Eliot and Auden should be continued, if necessary by joint authorship such as Beaumont and Fletcher or that inimitable pair Gilbert and Sullivan successfully achieved. The B.B.C. is still alive, and not quite so much asleep to poetry as it used to be; there is scope for the verse radio play and sketch on the lines laid down by Macleish and others, room for the ballad, the verse narrative, and the lyric, which have as much claim to the jazz-infested air and the echoes of the music-hall through suburban drawing-rooms as other, more dubious products of our civilization. Poets must begin to show, more definitely than ever, that they are reaching out to the vast audience which awaits them, and that they are capable of rising to the heroic level of the age in which they have become men.

December 1941.

A LETTER ON POETRY

DEAR TAMBI,

After many attempts at writing this letter I have at last decided to present only, with all the platitudes implied, some view of my present outlook on poetry, in the hope that you and your readers will correct and complete it.

I. *The Present Situation*

Asking ourselves why Byron and Shelley are better understood on the Continent than here, the answer is that the Continent has better understood the nature of Romanticism as a whole. The Romantic movement is not yet over, and in spite of ourselves we are a part of it. Graves with his dragons, Riding with her introspection, Eliot with his picture of social disintegration and isolation of the individual, Auden with his myths and slang, his revolt in both language and politics, the Sitwells with their making of music and fantasy; we are all in it up to the neck.

Coinciding with the French Revolution, Napoleon, the Industrial Revolution and a new conception of man, the Romantic movement was the logical outcome of a breakdown in a social and intellectual structure. Since then, no new synthesis has been achieved. The conditions under which Wordsworth and Shelley wrote are still with us. Romanticism did not die with the Revolution, because its revolutionary fervour was at once turned against the injustices of the machine age. It identified itself alternatively with the new socialism, or Anglo-Catholicism, or with the new aestheticism, branches of the same tree. I do not intend to develop this idea any more, beyond saying:

(*a*) that philosophy via Hegel, Bergson, Croce and Gentile has followed a line of romantic idealism;

(*b*) that the same applies to the modern individualist psychology of Freud and others;

(*c*) that the society which has been split by idealism and materialism is politically and culturally incapable of producing a synthesis.

II. *The Poet and his Age*

The poet at the present time is therefore in a difficult position. In literature alone, never mind society, he is faced by impossible alternatives: on the one side the reporting and materialist conception of Grigson and his group; on any other, the cultural synthesis recommended by Eliot and Pound; on another, he cannot open his mouth without being Right or Left (and automatically wrong for half the community); he has the alternative of the mumbo-jumbo of Surrealism (the prophetic Blake on a monstrous scale) or he is invited to be a little Dryden.

The air must be cleared: the only way at the present time is for the poet to realize his position and be himself. What is himself? Keats had the answer, which has been sadly mistranslated ever since he wrote it. He spoke of the poet 'having no character', 'negative capability'. By this he means that the poet must have every character: the character of the poet is his power of immense human sympathy. In as far as the poet realizes himself, he realizes all men. It is useless to condemn poets one does not understand: what has happened is that either the poet has not understood himself, or the critic has not understood the poet. In all cases the reader (whom no one obliges to read the poem) must in fairness give the poet the benefit of the doubt.

The 'self' of the poet at the present time is in a sense bound to be limited. The 'universal man' which was the ideal of the Renaissance no longer seems possible. No Leonardo could digest and reinterpret all the vast body of knowledge, all the thousand movements in society and art, which we have today. In any case, he addressed himself to a limited public which he knew and, 'universal' though in a sense he is, Leonardo was a great draughtsman and painter, and a minor poet.

The 'universal man' of our time would not, I think, be a poet. But supposing 'he' were: I think he would be rather a body of poets. Our poets, at present divided in hostile groups, are killing each other and writing one a wing, one a leg, one a beak, one an eye, of the bird of poetry. They must get together. One of the ways they can get together is in the verse-drama. I think that after the present war the verse-drama will be the medium through which some new synthesis in poetry might be achieved.

The poet at the present time is drawn between two seemingly irreconcilable conceptions of the universe: materialism and idealism. It should be realzed that these conceptions are only man-made and can be modified or overthrown. They are each a half-truth. Asked whether the universe is just matter, or whether it is just meaning, I reply that as far as I am aware it is both. This is the only answer to the materialists and the spiritual mystics. In common terms: there must be effected a synthesis between psychology and sociology. Auden tried to do it, in a rather too narrow way.

The poet must be of his age. As this age has been muddled, unpleasant, depressing, dishonest, so a great deal of poetry has had the same characteristics. But the fact that it has not all been so is a reply to those who regard poetry as an automatic secretion and reflection of the time. There has also been much honesty, much effort towards order. But the poet must be of his age, however bad the age may appear. If he is not 'modern' when he lives, if he is never contemporary when he is alive, he never will be contemporary. He will be still-born. That is why we don't want people to write Keatsian Odes, Shelleyan fables, Drydenian skits or Shakespearean tragedies of blood. We want these odes, fables, skits and tragedies to emerge from our present habits of thought and ways of living. All living poetry is contemporary, Shakespeare alongside of Eliot, Shelley alongside of Spender. If Spender modelled himself on Shelley he would not exist.

The poet must use the language of his contemporaries or one a little in advance of them. It is the only one he and they understand. It might be a useful exercise to write in the language of Chaucer: it would be more useful, however, to realize that Chaucer was using a language which in his own time was bright and new, not derivative and old. It is cheek to use foreign words when a good English equivalent exists. Look at Barker's early pseudo-miltonic diction, or Auden's pseudo-French in the 'New Year Letter'. I prefer a poet, like Dylan Thomas, to invent a word rather than borrow one. The same applies to imagery: perhaps there is something to be said for Scurfield's 'expensive bun' rather than the 'heavenly orbs' of the Hassall school. Have Wordsworth and Byron lived in vain? As for Keats, whom people throw at the modern poets, some of his worst poetry is a stew of cheap poetic diction, and his best poems are often good in spite of it. A writer like Bridges could digest a heavy poetic diction by amalgamating it with contemporary speech, of which he was a master. Let us finish with this snobbery of language: the word 'bun' is as fit for poetry as 'orb'; fitter, perhaps, since 'orb' is also one of those words which has become slightly funny. And the same with all the hollow words, the 'beauteous' and the ' wondrous' and what not.

III. *The Poet and Society*

All poetry is political and social, as are all men. But the social interpretation of poetry is only one of many, only one part of the critical act. Any criticism neglecting the social roots and radiation of poetry is incomplete. But the same applies to psychology, philosophy, aesthetics, religion, ethics, philology. Poetry reflects all human activities, and can be measured by them all.

Poetry is more than opinion. A Fascist and a Communist can both write a good poem about the present war. Human dignity must be observed.

There is no real difference between poetry and science. Science measures and discovers quantity ; poetry measures and discovers quality. But as there is no quality without quantity, the poet depends on the scientist, and poetry and science complete each other. Mankind will be delivered from ignorance and misery by the co-operation of the scientist with the artist.

Man is the measure of all things : poetry is the measure of man.

A poet is just a man who writes poetry. That is where the nineteenth century went wrong, in thinking he was something more than a man. We cannot accept Freud's idea of the poet as a freak. It is just as peculiar to make poems as it is to make tables or chemicals. Perhaps all men are freaks in this sense. But such a conclusion, which is highly questionable, would not differentiate the poet. We are all sensitive to different things and have all appropriate means of expression.

IV. *The Criticism of Poetry*

Real criticism of poetry must be done by poets. But

all men with special knowledge of human life can contribute to the tools of criticism. Parody, translation, imitation, satire, are the most direct forms of criticism. Criticism is choice. On its largest plane, criticism is thus right living. Criticism of poetry is learning to live with poetry.

Every poem is an integral, indivisible, infinite whole, like a person. Analyse a painting, and it is still there when you have done with it, only your knowledge of it is increased. Criticism increases knowledge. Analysing does not destroy poetry. Because in a sense one cannot analyse poetry: one can analyse only one's knowledge and understanding of it.

But every poem belongs to a greater unity, Poetry, as every man belongs to his species. All poetry co-exists. No mind which has not absorbed, felt and understood a wide range of poetry, can with impunity pass judgment on a new poem. That is why it is harder to grasp Dylan Thomas than Homer; not merely because of their own natures, but because the preparatory critical work has not been done.

Poetry can answer all man's needs, from uplift to amusement or even degradation. From the Epic, the moral treatise, to the smutty limerick. The hierarchy exists, not of size and intention, but of language and feeling.

V. *The Nature of Poetry*

All poetry is 'subjective'. There is a difference between a cat and a poem which is 'about' a cat. However objective a poet thinks himself, he can only present *more* or *less* than can be seen from looking at a cat. That which presents less is not art, though it might be journalism. That which presents more might be poetry or criticism, or just an auctioneer's catalogue. None the less we must love and cherish the Objective Reporters: they kept our feet on the ground. Let us love also the poets of the Apocalypse if they are any good: they help us to keep our head in the air.

Art is not entirely conscious or un- or sub-conscious. It is them all. We are all Surrealists sometimes. Nobody is a Surrealist all the time. Nobody is fully conscious all the time. Surrealism, like reporting, is a method of finding. After that it has to be purified. Surrealism has yet to be integrated into literature.

This brings us to Imagination. Imagination is an intuitive sense of reality. Imagery (and poetry itself) is the poet's expression, *simultaneously* in language, and in the most direct possible manner, of reality and his reaction to it. These two things must not be separate, as they sometimes are in defective poetry. Imagination can sometimes play the poet false, because every image, and every 'form', has an arbitrary element. What is inexact in the imagination can help us in other ways: that is why the Surrealists, though they do not always provoke pleasure, are sometimes able to throw light on our lives.

Imagination, like poetry, is neither transcendental nor miraculous. The scope of a man's imagination depends on his own life and experience. Imagination plays the same part in poetry as in dreams. Dreams are not whispered into our ears by little fairies.

Poetry is a complete human gesture. Psychologists, etc., disagree only about the origins of gestural expression (language). Language is simplified gesture, and poetry is simplified language. The gesture itself was originally the expression of a feeling or a thought. Thus we have the steps feeling–gesture–language–poetry. All the arts express life through a symbolic co-ordination of bodily functions. Poetry is a sort of dancing with the voice.

As in dancing, so in poetry: the most economical gesture is the most expressive. But flamboyant language will correspond with wild feeling, restrained language and rhythm with controlled feeling. We can judge a poet's sincerity only by such simple tests: if the language is prim while he talks about his heart breaking, then he is a bad poet, because he has not understood the appropriate gesture. Rhythm gives a lot away. The rhythm of a man's poetry should be both physical and psychic. Physically, it expresses the beat of his heart; psychically, it expresses the integration of his personality. Some rhythms we all know of, through which nothing but trivialities could be implied. But as for economy: economy in poetry is proportionate to the scale of the poet's nature. Blake, Hugo, and Shakespeare achieve their huge form of economy. The meanness of the economy of Pope and Gray reflects the small scale of their emotional lives: the poetic dwarf, and the other who had a 'white melancholy, a leucocholia', a negative feeling.

The greatest dishonesty is to express shapeless feeling in an artificially shapely way. I distrust a man whose heart breaks in faultless terza-rima. This is what is meant by 'academic' writing.

In writing all this I am in a sense betraying my belief that poetry should be treated empirically. Generalizations should spring only from the contemplation and analysis of individual poems. It is that method which, in criticism, I have adopted. It is a strange thing that we have had so many 'aestheticians' in this country who generalize glibly about poetry but have never proved that they could write anything worth reading about a poem. Everyone talks about poetry, but no one offers us a poem. But I think that any critic who has spent a life in writing and criticizing poetry would be able to contribute something to aesthetics, the theory of art (as I understand it, not 'the science of beauty' as some say). And the greatest task and privilege of the critic should be to sympathize. I agree with Dryden: 'They wholly mistake the nature of criticism who think its business principally to find fault.'

July 23rd, 1941.

A PERSONAL STATEMENT

WHILE my own development during the war—and in fact during my life—has been from defeatism to a complete acceptance of certain human truths and their relationship to writing, I am so conscious of having had a rather unusual background that the narration of my experience can serve as nothing more than a warning to those who ignore the problems of the individual in wartime. When I hear that So-and-so is in America, or that So-and-so-who-was-once-a-Pacifist is now working for the Ministry of Information, the news no longer excites me. Such apparent contradictions spring from the individual's own conscience and experience, and, while they are of great importance to society as a whole, they can be understood only by a sympathetic insight into each particular case. I take myself as a fairly typical instance of an attitude which might look to others like muddled thinking, but which I know to be deeply rooted in my childhood and education.

The third child of a marine engineer who was lost at sea in 1917, leaving a widow who was still suffering from the after-effects of meningitis, and myself suffering from rickets, after a few bitter-sweet years at home I was sent to a naval Orphanage where I spent four years. In that institution I was taught bayonet practice at the age of twelve, with a dummy rifle; learnt semaphore, how to hoist a flag, and for four years was marched about in military fashion along corridors, upstairs and downstairs, and had the number 107. I went to bed to the dying notes of the Last Post, and woke to the startling cry of the reveille, and marched to the dining-hall three times a day to the accompaniment of other bugle-calls whose

G

name I do not know. I learnt how to play a bombardon, but, being too small to carry it effectively, did not make enough progress to form part of the brass band which headed the uniformed boys on their way to church on Sundays. I developed an increasing admiration for France, which I knew only through Shakespeare's 'Henry V' and a geography book, and later I learnt French and became a lecturer on French literature. In spite of the hunger, the bullying, the route-marches, the fatigues, the fagging, the monotony, the uniform and the discipline, I still have tender feelings towards that institution where I learnt nothing, because at least it brought me into contact with all types of orphans, gave me a small-scale view of military life, increased my appreciation of home and the sea, helped me to realize that wars last a long time after they are over, and, above all, initiated me to the beauties of the country, trees, flowers and birds of all kinds, for the school was situated in vast, isolated grounds of its own which contained several farms. For present purposes, however, the important thing is that it taught me hatred of war. I often lay awake in the dormitory and thought of other orphans in France and Germany, and wondered whether they also had bugles and a brass band. Towards the end of my stay there I even went so far as to revolt against discipline, carrying on a liaison with a girl, to whom I passed letters, like Pyramus to Thisbe, through a wall, and whom I have never met to this day, and continued doing so after I had been found out and punished by various members of the staff. I had also started to write verse, which I used to scribble in the dormitory at night and show only to a weak boy with adenoids, threatening him with heavy penalties if he disclosed my secret.

By 1936 and '37 I was living in Paris, writing Surrealist verse, and was a temporary member of the French Com-

munist Party. I had been to three universities and a
secondary school without feeling really at home in any of
them. I abandoned both Surrealism and Communism in
1938, realizing the need for some more concentrated and
rational form of writing than Surrealism, and some
broader human values than those provided merely by
economics. Communism has, I think, been deformed
and cheapened by those hard-headed members who do
not realize that in such a movement idealists should be
able to breathe: they do not understand that a Stephen
Spender writing 'Man shall be Man' is doing something quite as important as an economist talking about
the Minimum Wage. When the Communists realize this
there will be some hope for a decent civilization in which
men will not be mere economic robots. As for Surrealism, it was logical enough that it should have attracted
me. Dadaism and Surrealism were symptoms of the
psychological illness of Europe; they were a defensive-
mechanism for the preservation of sanity. Feeling lost
and isolated in society, I sought these two types of
refuge: the dream-world (but with its materialist basis)
of Surrealism, and the human solidarity which Communism seemed to offer. I abandoned them both for
their narrowness.

Like many of my generation, I wrote more poems about
the Spanish war than about the present one, because then
we knew what was at stake, the idealism was obvious,
whereas in this war the M.O.I. has foolishly adopted a
negative attitude, has been unable even to define Democracy, and has spent too much time thrusting the burden
of the responsibility on to other people. We realized that
this war started in Spain, and perhaps that is why we had
grown defeatist by 1939. In my own case, for instance, I
had been a pacifist until 1936, and it is the realization of
the truths taught by the Spanish war—*that human values*

have to be struggled for—that changed my mind. That is why I do not object 'officially' to the present war.

As far as writing is concerned, I feel it is difficult to divorce it from reading. When war was declared in 1939 I was expecting to be called up. Like other people, I at once imagined myself as a soldier and wrote emotional poems about soldiers which have since caused me a great deal of amusement. That was not the way: although sincerely written, they do not satisfy. At the same time I also found that many of the poems I had hitherto admired no longer satisfied: I refer especially to the poems of the modern intellectuals. There seemed to have been far too many intellectuals merely scratching the surface of life. What I wanted was something which radiated feeling and meaning, not just bald statements, sketchy observations and trite commentaries. I found this deeper kind of writing in such poets as Dylan Thomas, Barker, Spender (those who, incidentally, have in some measure assimilated Surrealism and used it constructively), whose work I had hitherto neglected. I wrote an article on Thomas which brought me dangerously near an anti-intellectual conception of poetry, which I have since been trying to rectify. This led me to write a book on modern poetry, which helped me to realize my own solidarity with the writers of my generation. I find them all to some degree defeatist, all idealists longing for some better form of society. Most of them, like myself, have been consistently poor and have to struggle to make both ends meet. They are all in revolt against the business-man values, or lack of values, which have dominated our politics far too long and led to this new war. They have all tried dallying with some existing party, and have become extremists or have abandoned politics in disgust. Like mine, their minds have been torn between pacifist inclinations and the realization that this war is as necessary as the one in Spain. They are torn between despair at the present and hope for the future. They are tempted by intellectual rationalizations and by emotional escapism.

The main problem, as I see it, is that the younger writers must realize that *their critical position to contemporary society is not enough*. They warned and prophesied admirably and effectively before the war, but they wailed at the same time. Something more definite must be done if any positive literature is to be produced which will be in key with the people. How can this be done? Only by first of all realizing that the power of poetry is less local than that of a tommy-gun, knowing neither space nor time limitations. And, secondly, that concerted movement by writers could deal some smashing blows against injustice, and to hasten a better form of society. Less elegies, and a few more devastating satires. Satire is the most powerful weapon of the poet. We will need it. And above all, poetry must be richly emotional, must express all those inarticulate feelings of humanity, and stir men to courage and to action. I do not say this is all: poetry and art in general also exist for repose and contemplation.

All the above might suggest that I am giving dogmatic 'ends' to poetry which are exclusively social. That is not the case, for I cannot develop here other aspects of the problem as they should be developed. The war, more than anything, brought me to these conclusions. In my own poems I have expressed varying attitudes. The 'curve' might be indicated in this way: in 1939 I wrote a poem called 'Barcarolle' which expresses only the emotional chaos and horror of war. Then 'Conscript' ('Horizon', May 1940), which expresses the disorientation of the individual. In 'Letter to a Poet' I expressed the hope that a better future might arise from this war: in 'Seasons of War' I again returned to a sense of disillusion and frustration. My first 'positive' poem on the subject was 'Lines to a German', a short poem which appeared in the 'New English Weekly'. In the meantime I wrote several satiric poems, unpublished, and with the entry of Russia into the war wrote my first poem which sympathized with the war ('The Listener', July 31st, 1941). Or, I should say, not 'sympathized with the war' but with the human values which are at stake.

Meanwhile, the greatest change the war produced in me was to help me towards writing, with deeper feeling and sensual appreciation, lyrics about ordinary things and people. I regard these not as a measure of self-preservation, but also as a necessary part of the writer's job in a war: the preservation of all that is permanent and moving and simple in human life. Writing so-called 'war poems' is perhaps more 'useful', but less necessary than *a sensual understanding of human life and the human environment.*

What we need now, and will need after the war, will be some great mover of ideas, a sort of international Miskiewicz. I see no signs of one in this country, and do not seek the honour myself. He will no doubt be hounded through all the countries of Europe. But the question is: in what conditions can such an important poet emerge? Only, I think, when there is an immense rising of feeling, I do not mean a revolution, but an *emotional* upheaval, among the mass of the people. In this country such an emotional awakening is questionable, though here and there we see signs that it is not impossible. That Miskiewicz might be one man, but failing that, the young poets might collectively be one. They can do that by no longer wailing, but by forceful expression of the vital aspirations of humanity: love, economic stability, a belief in the sanctity of the human body and the inviolability of the mind, a belief in the liberation from humbug and hypocrisy of spontaneous human feeling. And on the negative side they must attack all the enemies of these aspirations, and have the courage to shout all injustice from the housetops. And in the meantime, before this collective Miskiewicz is suppressed, he will contemplate the fields and mountains, the miracles of human artistry, the faces of children, the singing of birds, the swelling of sails, the rain over cities, and all those ordinary miracles which make life worth living.

August 1941.

THE LIBERATION OF POETRY

'Poetry, London'

In 'Le Problème du Style' Rémy de Gourmont, that great impressionist critic who compensated for a lack of staying power by sure intuition and the finest of taste, was so bold as to divide writers into two types, which he called 'Emotive' and 'Visual'. Although the book caused some controversy in France, it was not realized that with these two words Gourmont foreshadowed a war of ideas, which is likely to rage for many years to come, between those who consider the poet as an individualist and those who see in him no more than an expression of the society which produced him. It is not on this side of the question that I wish to dwell, however, but on another, which has been already developed in the poetry and criticism of the past ten years: the degree to which reason and the emotions dominate the poet and his work. Let it be said at the outset that the struggle was unnecessary, for it should be evident, considering these words 'Visual' and 'Emotive', that art cannot spring from vision without emotion: this is already recognized in the relation of painting to photography. And it is equally true that emotion alone cannot create art unless it is guided and moulded by the intelligent mind. But the problem is not so simple as this, for a great poet, whose work lacks none of the qualities of feeling and sensual understanding, Paul Valéry, has on more than one occasion compared Poetry with Algebra, as Mallarmé did before him, while, on the other hand, the great rationalist writers of the Augustan age were for ever extolling Passion, for it was the age when one loved Newton and Locke, and wept over Pamela and Manon Lescaut.

Our country has never been rich in periodicals devoted to poetry, although there is hardly even a newspaper without its occasional poem, and poetry appears on publishers' lists as much for the air of cachet or of distinction it is supposed to give, as for reasons of esteem of the poets' importance. One can count the poetry reviews which have appeared in the last ten years on one hand, and it cannot be said that any of them was a paying proposition, although some of them gained wide appreciation. That is why it seems to me important that the two most successful of these, 'New Verse' and 'Poetry' (London), held diametrically opposed conceptions of poetry, conceptions which, indeed, fit very well under the two headings, 'Visuel' and 'Emotif', suggested by de Gourmont.

Enough has already been said of the direction of 'New Verse' (in the essays on Grigson, Allott and the Auden group) for us to dispense with any explanation of its doctrine. Grigson's injunctions have behind them a long ancestry, and might have been taken direct from Horace, from Boileau or Pope: 'nihil humani me alienum puto'; 'Aimez donc la Raison'; love Nature; 'What oft was thought', and so on. The appeals to common sense, however, were vastly different from those of the eighteenth century, for many new elements had been accumulated with time. From Wordsworth came the appeal for common speech; from Byron, the excuse for slang and much that was light; from Browning (and second-hand from Pound), an excuse for cramming one's own reading into poems; and the whole was complicated even further by T. S. Eliot's clinical imagery in 'Prufrock', or by that celebrated passage in one of his essays where Eliot argued that in the poet's experience there was no reason why the smell of cooking bacon (or was it steak?), the reading of Dante and the experience of falling in love should not co-exist. And what happened with these young poets was that a thousand and one experiences did co-exist in their verse, in a refreshing but alarming way which drove them far out of the track of their original Augustan models. Even the appeal for common speech went by the board when they digested James Joyce (and unwittingly Gertrude Stein at the same time) and fanned the precocious genius of Dylan Thomas. But one thing stood fast: the claim for exact reproduction of vision, or of experience (here again Wordsworth with his eye fixed steadily on the object came to their help), and the emphasis of this school lay on realism. That is why they preferred the late to the early Yeats, the young to the mature Eliot; that is why (apart from political considerations) their ardour for Day Lewis cooled as his capacity for emotional expression grew. But the amusing thing about their 'realism' was that they conveniently shut their eyes to Auden's development of Freud's (originally clinical) psychology into a mysticism of his own, just as most people in the 'thirties failed to see that there was a contradiction between the rational, materialist philosophy of the Surrealists and the irrational application of it. Nor did they attempt to reconcile their commonsense views with the mystic views of such poets as Rilke whom they so much admired. That is to say, there existed the same contradiction between the doctrine of 'New Verse' and the practice of its poets as there exists in any really healthy movement. We shudder to think what would have happened to so many young poets had they taken their prose utterances seriously. And it is this fact, that its prose was lively and its verse original, that made 'New Verse' worth reading.

But in a world where a Hemingway and a Virginia Woolf, a Dos Passos and a James Joyce, could exist at the same time, it was obvious that some reactions against the realist pretensions of 'New Verse' were bound to occur. They occurred when Roger Roughton founded 'Contemporary Poetry and Prose' and tried to dose a limited public with irrationalism; when Julian Symons founded 'Twentieth Century Verse' and gave a call to order, setting a premium on the traditional and literary conception of form and intellect; but the reaction was most evident when Tambimuttu's 'Poetry' (London) was founded, and set out on an emotional crusade against the matter-of-fact attitudes of Grigson and his friends.

In this country, where we still have the examples of Shelley, Blake, Wilde and Lawrence as a warning, he is a brave man who stands up to defend the senses and the emotions. He will at once be assailed by that puritanism which has been the staunchest support of common sense, restraint, decorum and reason for several centuries, and which only too often emanates from those who are afraid to live and unable to think. In this respect, our poetry, our poets, have had a strange fate. It is widely acknowledged that our poetry is one of the most human, one of the most rich in both reason and fantasy, one of the most exuberant in imagination, in the world, and that our language lends itself so well to verse that the poet can express many things in English which, in French for instance, would be indecorous or ridiculous in poetry. And yet, how timid have been our investigations into art, how chary we have been of claiming much for poetry, beyond its powers of ennobling the mind or purveying pleasure. On the Continent, a Hegel can claim for poetry all the realms of the spirit, into which mere reason cannot penetrate: a Vico can claim poetry as the harbinger and creator of religions: a Mallarmé can assert that poetry is a music of ideas (the phrase is mine, but that is what he meant): a Valéry can assert that Poetry is akin to Algebra, and people will listen and understand. Anyone making such claims in this country—as Shelley and Francis Thompson did—is at once denounced as mad. In Great Britain, where the marriage of Celt with Norman, Roman with Scandinavian, has produced a poetry of unparalleled wealth, every effort has been made to bring the eagle down to earth.   Poetry becomes, for us, a mere record, a mere photographic impression, a statement, an ambiguity, an image.   But now, after people have for so long been trying to pull poetry down to earth, there will be a determined attempt on the part of the younger generation to pull the earth up to poetry.

It might be that Tambimuttu has an exotic mind, but there can be no doubt that in his defence of the emotions, of the whole man, he has expressed fully the aspirations of a large body of the younger poets. His first 'Letter' on poetry was an explosive but reasoned manifesto, the drift of which can at once be shown by taking a few isolated statements, such as:

> Every man has poetry within him.
>
> Poetry is the awareness of the mind to the universe.
>
> The moment a man starts to write, he ceases to live.
>
> Man can transmit only a part of a whole vision at a given instant.
>
> No man is small enough to be neglected as a poet.
>
> Intellectualization is only half the truth.
>
> The trouble with the modern world is that it has no real beliefs or religion.   Poetry is religion.
>
> Poetry is a descent into the roots of life.

These phrases were to be a point of departure for a gradual elaboration of the broadest of doctrines, and above all it led to a determined effort to draw together as many of the poets as possible. Tambimuttu claimed in the second number that 'This paper . . . is a protest against the modern suppression of free speech in verse', and for a time it was a common thing to see De la Mare, Whistler, Dyment rubbing shoulders with Macneice and Spender, or Mallalieu side by side with an Apocalyptic poet. This was all good for poetry, and there is little doubt that such catholicity of taste in an editor can broaden the experience and stimulate the mind of his public.

In the third number the doctrine developed more fully with such statements as 'The birth of poetry is in the irrational, and the psychology of its appeal, like music, devolves finally upon the subconscious'. He was, to my mind, definitely on the right lines when he declared that 'The one real way of criticizing poetry is by the use of methods based on psychology', but I think there is a danger of carrying this too far, as he has done in subsequent numbers, basing many of his observations on Ortego Gasset and Jean-Jouve. Psychology, though it is one of the oldest human studies, is, as a science, still in its infancy, still in the theoretical stage. The clinical experiences of Freud, the examination of conscience, the study of apes, the psychology of the Gestalt, the mass-psychology of the school of Le Bon and MacDougall, Behaviourism— the fact that these approaches are so fertile, so convincing, and yet so contradictory, should lead us to beware of accepting psychology in its present state as the chief basis for criticism. Ever since the breakdown of the Historical and Impressionist schools of criticism, we have been at the mercies of the successors of Taine and Renan, for criticism in the twentieth century has assumed scientific pretensions of the most dangerous kind. Philosophy, Philology, were the thin end of the wedge, but criticism based on Marx and Engels, on Freud and Jung, while it has produced some startlingly interesting reading matter, has only too often missed the finer points of poetry and given imaginative writers a shabby deal. Two such instances of this are Dr Laforgue's book, 'The Defeat of Baudelaire', which successfully proved the poet a pervert of every kind, yet contributed little of value to our knowledge of poetry, and Alec West's study of Eliot and others. As for the psychological approach, we have only the psychologist's word for it that swords, the sea, moons and mountains are sexual symbols, for the trouble with them is that the very pens they write with, the paper they write on, and the ink they expend are equally of sexual importance. Psychology has still much advance to make before that synthesis can be produced which will enable us to apply it to our lives and our interests with any sureness. As for the sociological critics, we have only their word for it that poetry is good or bad according to whether the poet was Right or Left. Is it not strange that a Racine believed in Divine Right, or that Byron was a peer, that Blake had religious mania and D. H. Lawrence was an anarchist? Are we to believe that Vansittart is better than Kipling, or Paul Potts better than William Morris? Something other than 'The Right (or Left) ideas' is necessary before good poetry can be written. At the same time it is evident that as psychology and the social sciences advance, their results will prove increasingly valuable for criticism, provided that biology and so many other types of human research are brought to bear on the problem. The most a critic can do today, as at any other time, is to use his own judgment, while drawing his background as much as possible from contemporary thought in its many fields.

To return to the subject, it will be noticed that Tambimuttu throws great emphasis on the subconscious origins of poetry, and here he is rightly insisting on an aspect of modern psychological investigation which the 'New Verse' poets have tended to overlook, and I know of no fairer estimate of Surrealism than he has made: 'The Surrealist movement was the most important, and the only one properly belonging to the age, and would have done more for the health of modern verse had it possessed more poets of major importance' ('Poetry', No. 4). From Plato onwards, there have always been philosophers ready to plead the cause of inspiration, which they have ascribed to madness, divine or satanic intervention, magic, and other extraordinary powers. Today, when we can with some certainty speak of the subconscious mind, we are in a position to regard the writing of poetry of any kind as rational behaviour, without sacrificing any of its extraordinary properties. This discovery, however, has not yet penetrated men's minds, and they do not realize that great tracts of human consciousness remain to be explored, and that poetry, in which the conscious and subconscious minds are in the closest contact possible in any human form of expression, has a great part to play in the liberation of man from the so-called 'logic', the so-called 'principles', the so-called 'reason' which have been built up largely on the observation of facts external to man. A few months ago, a number of the Indian P.E.N. bulletin recorded that a Professor in India had referred, in his inaugural lecture, to my article on Dylan Thomas, and had expressed some puzzlement that mankind might yet be saved (as I did not claim it would be) by such expression of the deeper realities of the human mind and the emotions. The answer is clear: mankind will not be saved by this or by that, but if it is to be saved, it will be only by a poetry, a conception of society, a religion, an idealism, which will permit the complete liberation of man from the chains of prejudice, the dry bones of logic, the inhibition of the primal instincts, the thwarting of emotions, the enslaving of the body to highly artificial modes of life. What we now want of poetry is that it shall be written with the whole mind, the whole body, the whole soul, and there can be no hope for a society in which this remains to a large extent impossible. This, I think, is what Herbert Read meant when he wrote: 'Poets should not go outside their own ranks for a policy; for poetry has its own politics' ('Poetry', No. 5).

There is no space here for an analysis of the direction of 'Poetry' (London), other than the above examination of some of its editor's arguments. But it can be stated definitely that there has not been a review since the Great War which has gathered so many poets into its pages. Almost all the poets mentioned in this book have appeared in it, and there are many more well worth detailed study, such as Lawrence Durrell, D. S. Savage, Audrey Beecham, Charles Madge (a 'New Verse' poet also) and Ruthven Todd. To conclude, I leave the reader with a phrase by D. S. Savage which appeared in the first number of 'Poetry', and which seems to me to embody the most widespread feeling among the younger poets at the present time. It sums up not only the outlook of the magazine we have been considering, but also the idea which will bear most strongly on poetry in the next few years: 'Apart from the consideration of pure genius, or heavenly aspiration, what a poet writes depends upon what he *is*, upon the degree of personal integration he has achieved by moral effort and disciplinary training of his faculties.' Or, as Julian Symons has written, art is an autobiographical game. Or, in the words of Boileau some two hundred and fifty years ago, 'Le vers se sent toujours des bassesses du cœur' (Each line reveals the baseness of the heart). The poet will heal the wounds of humanity only by reaching deeply into himself, and by expressing his inner vision with fearless sincerity.

December 1941.

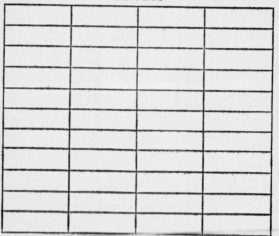